YOLO

Lessons Learned From Eve & Esther

Denalee Call Chapman

With gratitude to Heavenly Father for the gift of life.

PREFACE

PREFACE

YOLO: A popular colloquialism. Many of you may have heard it, some of you may hear it regularly from your kids. It means "You Only Live Once." Although for a good year, my daughter, Azure, believed it meant "You Only Love Oreos." (The girls in our family are pretty gullible. In fact, I believed for a long time that the HOV lane on freeways were for Hybrid Operated Vehicles only – because that's what someone told me.) Back to YOLO – We really do only live once on this earth. Life is made up of moments, each of which cannot be reclaimed. The moment comes, and then the moment is gone. We use it – or we lose it. How are we living our moments? Do we remember YOLO?

During one 12-year period our family lived in Alaska. When we moved there we had 4 kids; the two youngest were ages one and two. I was a busy mother, but loved that life! We lived in a small town on a big island, surrounded by ocean and mountains and all the things you think of when you hear "Alaska." Although there was lots of ocean, there weren't many kid-friendly beaches. There was one though – for obvious reasons it was called Sandy Beach. When the tide was low, the sand would be exposed and it would call to all the locals to come hang out. We found out, that first summer, that it was a rare day when the tide was low **and** the sun was out. When that happened, Sandy Beach become the hot spot of Sitka. One of those beautiful summer days, my husband, Brad, was home with the kids and so I snuck out for a bit of time alone. By the time I got to the beach, families were on the way out because the sun was disappearing behind clouds. I was alone on the beach … It was quiet, it was still, it was peaceful. The tide had started coming in, so I parked myself right where the sand met the rocks to give me maximum time. I got comfortable, opened my book and relaxed. Before I started to read, I just closed my eyes and listened. Distant kid sounds, the breeze mixed with the surf ... Oh how peaceful! I opened my book to read and I was just so relaxed that I got only about a page into the book, shut it, and then closed my eyes again. As I was lying there I reveled in the joy of motherhood, in the beauty of nature, and in the goodness of Heavenly Father. I didn't want to sleep – just enjoy and relax. Before long, I sat up and gazed at the scenery. Every now and then I'd stop staring at the ocean and look around at the rest of nature. But my eyes were always drawn back to the ocean. It was mesmerizing – staring at the water, watching the waves come in, then pull out. I loved listening to the unique sounds of the water coming toward me, then being sucked away again. For the life of me, it really looked like the tide must be falling – it would come in, then it would pull out SO far! But all of a sudden I was pulled out of my stupor as the water touched my toes! I had no idea the tide was coming in so quickly. It didn't look like it was making any progress at all. I had felt like I could stay on the beach forever and nothing would change. I gathered my things and went home. But the experience stayed with me. Those moments at the beach – they felt like they were frozen in time. I didn't think any time was passing at all ... and yet, it had. The tide had come in and I didn't even notice!

Our lives are like that. Sometimes it seems like we will be in our current stage of life forever – just like the tide, we know, in our minds -   it will eventually change, but sometimes we're blindsided when all of a sudden we realize we're not in our 20s anymore! Or we no longer pack a diaper bag for every outing;

or there aren't enough kids still at home to go through a gallon of milk a day. Whatever our surprise moments of time passage are, we've all had them. It's shocking, really, to know that the tide has come in – when we've been watching it all along and it hadn't seemed to change at all.

YOLO is more than just a popular, trendy word. It's a good reminder to live in the moment. Remembering the past and planning for the future is important. It's vital, really. But not at the expense of losing our moments.

I am fascinated with Eve and with Esther. Their examples of embracing "YOLO" are worth emulating.

We don't know how long Eve and Adam were in the Garden of Eden before making the choice of mortality. But the fact that it took any time at all to choose to move forward tells me that they loved their moments in the Garden. It tells me that Eve made the most of her time there. And then, once she decided and acted, the journey began. Do you think Eve sat around moping about having left the Garden? Do you think she couldn't get past it to the point of not enjoying "the moment"? I don't. And I have scriptural proof: "Were it not for our transgression, we never should have had seed, and never should have known good and evil, and the joy of our redemption, and the eternal life which God giveth unto all the obedient." (Moses 5:11) Eve didn't need a teenager to shout: YOLO. She instinctively lived it.

Esther was a woman of similar joyful integrity. She lived in the moment, grateful for her past, and grounded regarding the future. But she lived in the present, unafraid. She was confident. She was cheerful. She was good.

What characteristics did Eve and Esther share that made them women to be emulated? How can we become more like Eve and Esther? Our lives are made up of years; years made of days; and days made up of moments. Living in the moment is a choice. Living *joyfully* no matter what the moments bring, is an attribute that can be cultivated and a gift of the Spirit.

Living in the present and being joyful shows gratitude to our Heavenly Father for the gift of mortality. And it makes our mortal adventure so much more enjoyable and properly memorable.

If we are intentional about our time, the day will come when we will feel fulfilled and satisfied because we savored our moments. YOLO.

CHAPTER 1
OUR NEED FOR EACH OTHER

We need each other. No matter how independent we think we are, none of us is meant to go through life without lifting others and being lifted by others. As brothers and sisters on this Earth, we are all connected. Everything we do affects not only ourselves, but others around us as well. Part of being true to YOLO is to recognize the need for others, as well as the effect we all have on each other, every moment of our lives.

While Eve was with Adam in the Garden of Eden, we know the two of them spent time in the presence of Heavenly Father. And they spent much time with each other. We don't know how long they were in the Garden before making the choice to step into mortality, but we know that the time they were in the Garden was, in every sense, heavenly.

Marjorie Pay Hinckley said, "We are all in this together. We need each other. Oh, how we need each other. Those of us who are old need you who are young, and hopefully, you who are young need some of us who are old...We need deep and satisfying and loyal friendships with each other. These friendships are a necessary source of sustenance." (Virginia H. Pearce, ed., Glimpses into the Life and Heart of Marjorie Pay Hinckley (1999), 254–55) And so I think of Eve and her husband in the Garden of Eden. I wonder about her associations and can't help but believe that Eve was not only instructed (along with Adam) by Heavenly Father, but I believe she also had angel friends with whom she visited.

Having been foreordained to be "the mother of all living" (Moses 4:26) I'm certain that Eve studied and pondered and had great need to discuss her upcoming choice. Surely, she and Adam not only enjoyed a peaceful atmosphere in the Garden of Eden, but they also had some serious discussions about partaking of the fruit. Not having yet become mortal, there was so very much that they could only imagine. I'm sure that many of their conversations included what the future would hold. And I'm sure that Eve enjoyed the perspective from her Heavenly Mother and her angel friends.

Adam and Eve weren't alone in the Garden and they weren't alone once they fell. We know of visits from Heavenly messengers. Elder Jeffrey R. Holland taught, "When Adam and Eve willingly stepped into mortality, they knew this telestial world would contain thorns and thistles and troubles of every kind. Perhaps their most challenging realization, however, was not the hardship and danger they would endure but the fact that they would now be distanced from God, separated from Him with whom they had walked and talked, who had given them face-to-face counsel. After this conscious choice, as the record of creation says, 'they saw him not; for they were shut out from his presence.' (Moses 5:4) Amidst all else that must have troubled them, surely this must have troubled them the most. But God knew the challenges they would face, and He certainly knew how lonely and troubled they would sometimes feel. So He watched over His mortal family constantly, heard their prayers always, and sent prophets (and later apostles) to teach, counsel, and guide them. But in times of special need, He sent angels, divine messengers, to bless His children, reassure them that heaven was always very close and that His help was always very near. Indeed, shortly after Adam and Eve found themselves in the lone and dreary world, an angel appeared unto them (Moses 5:6-8) ..." (*The Ministry of Angels, October 2008 General Conference*)

Adam and Eve didn't go it alone ... none of us do.

When we are able to recognize how often others have an effect in our lives, that is when we will realize how important we may be to others. Most of the time we won't know the impact we've had on other people. But sometimes we are rewarded with a sweet glimpse into the life of another, and see clearly our role in helping.

It was a Sunday afternoon – nearly evening. A typical Sunday, we had been filled with the joy of the Sabbath and were just settling down. Full tummies, and time for pajamas. My husband and son had taken our one family car and I was home with the girls. Standing at the kitchen sink I had the feeling to call a particular friend. I knew she had family in town, so was hesitant. But I've learned through the years that promptings that are followed result in peace; not followed – they create uneasiness. So I called. The phone rang and rang and rang. Just as I was expecting a voicemail message, my friend answered. But I could hardly tell it was her. "Denalee," she sobbed.

"Are you ok? What is wrong? I need to help you. Please tell me what you need," I begged. She couldn't answer. I spoke: "I'll be right there." So I hung up the phone, put on a pair of sneakers, and told the girls where I was going. I ran out the door and didn't stop running until I got to her home just a mile or so away. When I arrived, we embraced and then she explained. "I had to talk with you. I was on my knees in prayer, pleading for direction. I didn't know how to approach you – and then you called. You acted; I didn't have to." She then proceeded to share what she needed to with me.

We struggled with infertility through our childbearing years. Eventually all five of our children were born – one of them, we adopted. Bryan was born on the island of Guam while we lived there. We had Bryan in our foster care from 5 weeks of age, and made it known to Guam Social Services that we wanted to adopt him. When he was 8 months old, parental rights were terminated and he became adoptable. When the agency contacted us, we were ecstatic! But before the conversation was over, they made it clear that we were not being considered as his adoptive family. They thought it would be in Bryan's best interest to place him in a family with brown skin.

At this time, my parents were serving a mission in British Columbia. This was in the day when we wrote letters and only made phone calls on special occasions – they were just too expensive, especially internationally. But we were devastated. I called the home number where my parents were staying and left a slightly detailed message with the sweet older woman whose home it was. When my parents returned that evening, they called. My mom comforted me, advised me, and offered appropriate empathy. Then she told me that Ivy Rose, the homeowner, shared with her that as soon as she got off the phone with me, she dropped to her knees and prayed in our behalf.

We had people all over the world praying for us – people of all denominations. Most of those people were made aware when things turned in our favor and Bryan's adoption was finalized. But most heard through other people – those who had shared our plight with them. I know there were many people who I didn't even know about praying for us. And so, our gratitude was spoken in prayer to Heavenly Father, for those good people who exercised faith in our behalf. But years later I attended a BYU Women's Conference. My parents were presenting and so I had the sweet opportunity of walking around with them to meet people they knew. One of those was Shirley Burnham, the bishop's wife in one of the areas they served in while on their mission. When my mom introduced me, Shirley said, "Denalee ... oh how we prayed for you!" I was overcome with a love and a sense of gratitude so deep that tears just poured out of my eyes. To be able to thank, face-to-face, one whose prayers and faith contributed to the formation of our eternal family was a sweet gift, indeed. Shirley had made a difference in my life. And I was able to thank her.

Our lives on this Earth are so interconnected! We truly need each other. Sometimes we will know the effect our actions have on another, sometimes not. And sometimes we will be able to thank those who have touched our lives – and sometimes not. But just knowing that every person we come in contact with helps to shape us, and we them ... it gives us not only a sense of belonging and comradery, but also a sense of responsibility.

Eve had to have felt a great responsibility to all of humankind. She must have known that what she would eventually choose to do would make life hard for her. But she also knew that it was the only way to fulfill her divine destiny.

Each of us has a divine destiny. And just as with Eve, the fact that we have been foreordained and have a divine path *does not* take away our agency. We each have the blessing of choice. Sometimes our choices seem clear. And sometimes our choices are relatively easy. But sometimes, what lies ahead of us seems daunting, like it must have sometimes seemed to Eve. Sometimes, as we prepare to choose, we are filled with a mixture of excitement and concern – both at the same time.

Esther's experience recorded in the Bible is one of those that I imagine filled her with contrasting feelings. I think about darling, young, Jewish Esther, growing up with loving parents. And I imagine her sadness as her parents passed away and she was alone. And then her developing relationship with Mordecai who adopted her and was a mentor and positive influence in so many ways. You'll remember that the King was displeased with his wife. She refused his orders to come out and show her beauty, and so he divorced and dethroned her. The king, at the suggestion of his council, gathered the beautiful young virgins of his kingdom … it's sort of a fairy tale, Cinderella-like story. They all come to the palace and live together for a year in a state of "purification." We read that Esther "obtained favor in the sight of all them that looked upon her." She was not only the King's favorite – thereby becoming the new queen – but she was also a favorite of all of her competitors and the servants …everyone who knew her. When I think of Esther I think of someone whose inner beauty bursts through and makes her unmistakable outward beauty almost magical. She couldn't help but have friends. I think Esther must have been a woman of great confidence – confidence that can only come from righteous living. Modern scriptures advise us: "Let thy bowels also be full of charity toward all men … and let virtue garnish thy thoughts unceasingly; then shall thy confidence wax strong in the presence of God … the Holy Ghost shall be thy constant companion, and thy scepter an unchanging scepter of righteousness and truth …" (D&C 121: 45-46) Surely Esther's charity toward others and her virtue gave her the confidence she needed to fulfill her divine destiny. A destiny which would save the Jewish people in her day. And so Esther, who made it through the 12-months of purification, who found favor with all the other women, and who became the King's bride and Queen of all, never forgot who she was. When Mordecai got the message to her that scheming Haman was going to have all the Jews killed, Esther was faced with an impossible choice.

I think Esther's choice was similar to Eve's choice. In both cases, in order to provide life, these courageous women would have to leave their personal comfort. They had to forget themselves and accept the possibility of death so others could have life. I'm certain that Eve prayed for direction, counseled with her husband, enlisted the help of angels — before executing her decision to partake of the fruit. And we know that Esther counseled with Mordecai and then enlisted the help of friends and family as they fasted and prayed together before executing her decision to approach the King. In the end, both women fulfilled the part Heavenly Father desired of them. As Mordecai told Esther, "… who knoweth whether thou art come … for such a time as this?" (Esther 4:14)

Our roles are equally essential to the salvation of ourselves and others as Eve's and Esther's were. And we are, each of us, our brother's brother or sisters' sister. Whether we are placed in a calling of responsibility or not, as members of The Church of Jesus Christ of Latter-day Saints, and particularly for sisters, as members of the Relief Society, we have the privilege of loving, serving and saving each other. We are particularly responsible for those we are assigned to Home Teach and to Visit Teach. Because I am a member of the Relief Society, my experiences are mainly with Visiting Teaching. Let me share some experiences that might illustrate how small acts of fulfilling visiting teaching assignments and other responsibilities in Relief Society have made a difference:

I served my mission in Japan about a million years ago. My second area was the one area in the mission that everyone hoped to avoid. They hadn't had a baptism there in as long as anyone could remember. And the branch of 80 or so people had only 15 or 20 people attending each week. It was the "arm pit" of the mission. I moaned and groaned and whined about being sent to Tokorozawa. Well, once I got over myself and started to concentrate on my responsibility and on serving the Lord, my companion and I felt inspired to start visiting teaching – I think the branch had reported 0% visiting teaching for the previous several months. Well, we got a list of members and began visiting. As best as I can remember, every sister we visited was thrilled to see us and said something like, "I thought the church had forgotten about me." The visiting teaching snowballed as we'd then take the newly visited sister with us to visit another "forgotten" one. And by the time I left that area a few months later, the meetinghouse was filled with attendance at around 50 people each Sunday. These sweet sisters just needed to be remembered. And then they needed to be needed. Fast-forward 20 years. I walked in to the church on a Wednesday night and picked up a copy of the Church News that was sitting in the foyer. Waiting for my husband, I sat on the sofa and flipped through it. On the back pages were the announcements of new Stake Presidents. I was filled with shock and gratitude when I read of a newly called Stake President in the Tokorozawa 2nd Stake. Two stakes, in a mission area that had fewer than 20 people attending church when I was there. I

18

can't help but believe that visiting teaching had something to do with that.

When I was 17-years-old I graduated high school and left my family in Pennsylvania to attend Ricks College in Idaho. It was an exciting time and I loved being a part of the Relief Society. Student life was fun (at least it was fun for me … I had no idea what major I wanted, so I took classes like Modern Dance, Anatomy & Physiology, and Interior Design), but of course I missed family life. In Pennsylvania there was a missionary from Rexburg. When he found out I'd be attending Ricks, he gave me his parents' address and suggested I look them up. They became family to me and my roommates. Their missionary son, the youngest of two children, had just left home so they were empty-nesters and seemed to enjoy visits from silly teenage girls. About once a week we'd stop in and either have dinner together, or eat freshly baked cookies while we took a break from our real lives. Brother and Sister Moore were gentle, completely genuine individuals whom we all grew to love. Years flew by, as they do, and my oldest daughter began attending BYU-Idaho. Thrilling to me, she moved in to the exact same apartment I lived in my first semester. While at school she met and married a wonderful man and they started their family. They moved into a darling little house and Brooke became the Compassionate Service Leader. She was made aware of a woman in a nursing home within the ward boundaries, and was asked to visit her monthly. Together, Brooke, Steve and their little boy, Gage, made the plan to go visit. It was cold … really cold. If you've ever been in Rexburg in the winter, you know that the wind and snow is enough to send you straight back inside! Brooke told me that it was one of those things she knew she needed to do, and it never left her mind – sort of nagged at her. When they finally made the plans to go, Brooke says, "Life slowed down for us. We went out in the winter weather to the nursing home, and it felt good." For this busy little family, going to school and working – trying to make ends meet, as students do – visiting the nursing home was kind of a *sigh of relief*. Well, they were escorted up to the sister's room, which Brooke says, felt very much like a home in itself. With personal knick-knacks and photos all around, the smell of homemade cookies – it was comfy and cozy in a Mrs. Weasley sort of way. They felt immediately welcomed. The sister was a gracious and regal host, and although at her age, there wasn't much that she could do, she did her best to make this young family feel at home. She offered little Gage homemade cookies and hard old-lady candies, and Gage was comfortable. For Brooke and her family, the feeling of visiting this sister in the nursing home was like entering the temple. They left their busy "must-do" things and entered a new dimension. Life was slow, there was time to just visit without cares. And they did visit. The epicenter of the room was a large picture of this sister's husband. So they asked about him and it was clear that he was also the epicenter of her life. She talked about his going back to school as an older man and being the oldest to ever graduate from Ricks College. She talked about the 30 or so years he was home teacher to the Eyrings – yes, President Eyring's family – and what a sweet experience that was for him. In that visit to this sister, Brooke's family was blessed. They were blessed by her wisdom, the peace she carried with her, and her acceptance of them. Brooke called me the next day and told me about the visit. She said she was assigned to visit Sister Moore in the nursing home, and what a blessing to her and her family that they did it. "Sister Moore?

Was it Lila Moore? What was her husband's name? Craig? Brookie! This is the Sister Moore who blessed my life so many years ago!" Brooke had gone, by assignment, to bless the life of Sister Moore, but left a happier, more blessed person herself. And I was blessed by Brooke's visit – as I recalled the joy Sister Moore gave to me.

Have you ever heard of "the casserole syndrome" in relation to Visiting Teaching? My sister recently told me about it – you know, *I'll just make a casserole, drop it off and say, "let me know if I can do anything for you."* ...That's the casserole syndrome. Well, my sister Jennilyn had a visiting teacher once who went beyond the casserole syndrome. Back in the old days, the weeknight activity was almost always a crafting event. Jennilyn doesn't think she's any good at crafts (I think she is) and so would always come home dissatisfied with her project. She'd still attend, because it was the right thing to do, but month after month she would come home discouraged with herself and thinking less of herself because of the craft that she always thought was a flop. This one Wednesday night they were making something – a paper towel holder or something – that they would paint a teddy bear face onto. Jennilyn watched in a mixture of despair and admiration as her visiting teacher, across the table from her, drew her own teddy bear and prepared to paint it. Jennilyn exercised some courage and asked her to please draw the face on hers as well. Then she told her how she felt about all of the crafts she took home, and how she felt about herself after each activity. Jennilyn's visiting teacher not only drew the teddy bear on Jennilyn's project, but also offered to paint it for her. She still has it. She doesn't use it, except to pull out every now and then to remind herself of her testimony of visiting teaching. It goes beyond casseroles and empty offers. True visiting teaching is stepping in and helping in the unique ways those you visit need help.

I witnessed a home teacher really finding and filling a need recently. I was spending a few days with my sister and her family out of state. It was a Sunday night and my flight was leaving super early the next morning. The home teacher called to see if he could stop by, and in our family we're really jealous of our time together. So when my sister told him, on the phone, that she didn't want to take any time away from me, he asked if there was anything they needed. She said, "As a matter of fact, my sister's laptop has a virus. Can you help?" That good home teacher came over and spent the next two hours visiting with my brother-in-law as he worked tirelessly to de-bug my computer. And then he went the extra mile again. A couple of days after I returned home he sent an email to my brother-in-law with instructions to pass on to me to get even better results. Now, that's good home teaching! He gave a real service, and also allowed my sister to be with me rather than having us all sit down and listen to his message.

My mom told me about her visiting teaching during my teenage years. We had just moved to Pennsylvania – my mom was in her early 40s and she had been assigned to visit teach a woman approaching 80. She's not sure she ever felt intimidated by it, but she did wonder at it. The sister's name was Orpha Heinselman and her daughter, Dodie Gross was also in our ward. Dodie was in her 50s, so to me, she was an old woman herself. ☺ Well, my mom and Orpha became such good friends that when any of the ladies were getting together, even if Dodie was unavailable, they would still invite Orpha – she was just so much fun. My mom remembers Orpha telling her, "It's so nice to have someone call me by my first name." I'm reminded of Sister Hinckley's statement I shared at the start of this chapter – we all need each other. It doesn't matter our age.

In another area my mom was assigned to be a visiting teaching companion with Lenore Romney, who was 20-30 years older than she was – they served together for 6 years. There was a bit of a distance to drive to visit the sisters in that area, so they had time for talking and learning from each other. My mom learned from her companion – from her wisdom and her life experiences. The greatest thing Sister Romney taught my mom was on one of those drives – she said, "I just adore my husband! Don't you adore your husband?" It got my mom thinking – *Yes! She did adore her husband. But did she show it? Did he know?*

Coincidentally, my sister, as a young married, moved into that ward and was immediately assigned to visit teach Sister Romney. Jennilyn's companion didn't make any arrangements to get together, and Jennilyn, new to the ward, a young married, and understandably intimidated to visit Lenore Romney, just sat back and waited. A couple of months after being assigned, Sister Romney walked up to her in church and said, "Jennilyn, you are my visiting teacher. And I NEED YOU to come!" We need each other, sisters.

Not only does our age not matter when it comes to needing each other, but it also doesn't matter our level of activity in the church. Are any of you old enough to remember the big gas crunch in the 70s? It got so bad that the President lowered the speed limits on the freeways to 55. Well, at that time, when you could only get gas on certain days, and the amount was limited, some of the families in our ward were told that because of the distance we lived from everyone else, the sisters in that area would not be getting visiting teachers. My mom told me that she thought, *Oh that's fine … I don't really need visiting teachers*. But as the months went on, she felt a huge loss. She felt forgotten, to a degree. **She did need visiting teachers**. It didn't matter that she lived far away or that she was completely active. She needed visits from sisters, and she needed to know she was thought about and important. We all do.

The visiting teaching assignments I've had in the various wards I've lived in have been gifts to me. Our Relief Society Presidents, Elders Quorum Presidents, High Priest Group Leaders and Bishops are inspired. They pray and ponder and pray some more over the constantly changing visiting assignments. I am so grateful for Relief Society presidents who have been connected to the Spirit as they've given me my assignments. I can't think of a single time I've visited without coming away uplifted myself. I've wondered and marveled at the gift that visiting teaching is to the one assigned to do the visiting – in my case, so much more for me than for those I visit. My testimony of visiting teaching grows each time I fulfill the assignment. And so I wonder: Why is it *so difficult* to do this one little thing? With all the other monumental things we, as LDS men and women do – so many of those things on a daily basis, why, oh *why* is it so hard to visit our sisters or our families just once a month? Well, the answer is obvious – the effect of small monthly visits is so great that Satan does all he can to stop them. He fills our lives with other things and whispers to us that "skipping it this month won't matter." Before we know it, home teaching and visiting teaching then become guilt trips instead of the blessings that they are meant to be.

I mentioned Brooke earlier – she told me recently about a time, nearly a year ago, when she was in a huge funk. She just couldn't seem to pull herself out of it. Out of duty, she went visiting teaching. The act of obedience to that assignment was just the medicine she needed. It wasn't a particularly inspirational visit – nothing noteworthy, but when she left, the heaviness Brooke had been plagued with was lifted.

As I've been blessed by visiting teaching, I ask myself of those who have influenced me, "… who knoweth whether [she has] come … for such a time as this?" There have been women in my life who have "saved" me every bit as much as Esther saved her Jewish brothers and sisters. Lest we forget, working toward eternal lives is the real purpose of our moments of life. And when we use some of our moments to lift others toward their exaltation, we are rising as well. When Eve made her choice in Eden and gave life to us all, that very act lifted her toward her exaltation. When Esther acted in behalf of all the Jews of her time, although she was risking her mortal life, she was saving her eternal life.

It was Lucy Mack Smith who said, "We must cherish one another, watch over one another, comfort one another and gain instruction, that we may all sit down in heaven together." As we move forward starting today, with the rest of our lives, let's consider taking YOLO as a personal motto. And as we do, remember that everyone we come in contact with will influence us, and we have a responsibility to lift them as well.

CHAPTER 2
DON'T SWEAT THE SMALL STUFF

Even as an adult I still need to be reminded to not "sweat the small stuff." Not long ago, while visiting my elderly parents, I was disappointed in myself when I realized I was allowing something relatively inconsequential to get at me. In the scheme of things, I knew it was so miniscule that I should just let go of it – and I vowed to do so. And then … I let the fact that I had been bothered by something so small eat at me. It was an irrational downward spiral I had begun. I confided in my father, the one who always reminded us: *Don't sweat the small stuff*, and he helped me snap out of the cloudy, unreal reality that I had created for myself. He told me, "That little thing you recognize as 'small stuff,' but you may want to consider classifying your letting it bother you as 'small stuff' as well." I realized then that Heavenly Father does want us to recognize our shortcomings and work on them; but He doesn't want us to brew them, carefully stirring our pot of sins. He wants us to recognize the wrong, determine to change, and then move forward.

After Eve and Adam had partaken of the forbidden fruit, knowing that they were gifting their spirit brothers and sisters with a mortal experience that would be the means of progression for us all, I suspect they may have also felt some concern for what the future may hold. They became mortal and were then able to see in a way they hadn't before. There would be consequences for their actions – they knew that. Scripture reveals little of what Adam and Eve did after partaking of the fruit. We know they "sewed fig leaves together, and made themselves aprons." (Genesis 3:7) And we know that it was while they were "walking in the garden in the cool of the day" that "they heard the voice of the Lord God." (Genesis 3:8) I love the imagery here. I love imagining Eve walking with her husband and the two of them talking about what they've learned, and what their future might be. I know that as they walked together in the cool of the day, their conversation had to have been righteous and joyful – not condemning of each other or contentious; not filled with worry and doubt. Or else, how could they have heard the voice of the Lord? I don't think Eve was biting her nails, focusing on little things that really don't matter. I don't think she was berating herself or blaming her husband. I think she and Adam were planning and preparing. I think they were looking forward with an eye of faith, knowing that the future would be tough but that they would be made strong as they grew bit by bit. Eve is an example of preparing and acting; doing hard things with the broad picture in mind; of not sweating the small stuff.

"Don't sweat the small stuff" doesn't mean don't pay attention to detail. In fact, it's details carefully executed that create a successful result. Such is the case with Esther and Mordecai. "Don't sweat the small stuff" really means, "have faith and let the Lord help you through the details." Esther knew that approaching the king's inner court without an invitation meant death. Unless, of course, he would hold out his golden scepter. She didn't haphazardly walk into the court just hoping she wouldn't be killed. Esther didn't "sweat the small stuff" – that is, she didn't anguish over all the things that could go wrong. Instead, she made a plan. A plan which included others, but most importantly, required faith and divine intervention. All the while, Esther trusted in Heavenly Father's will. Remember that after petitioning her maidens as well as all the Jews in the area to fast with her, she told Mordecai, "... and so I will go in unto the king, which is not according to the law: and if I perish, I perish." (Esther 4:16)   Esther looked at the situation, considered the possibilities, made a plan, then moved forward in faith with a desire to be aligned with Heavenly Father's will.

I am an expert at sweating the small stuff! In fact, it began when I was just a baby. My very first memory is as a baby in church. This is true – my mother corroborates it! I had to have been less than a year old. Two things stand out from that day: 1) the dress my mom was wearing scratched my chin as I rested my chin on her shoulder; and 2) the big, mean, scary ladies in the row behind us passed me back and forth between each other as I screamed to go back to my mommy. (Funny how I can remember that, but I cannot, for the life of me, remember what I ate yesterday!)

Fast forward: I was in 1st grade. My teacher was Mrs. Wadlow – and oh! How I loved her! At the end of the school year, one day after school she invited me up to her desk to pick out something I could keep. It was such a hard decision, since I could only pick one thing. There was a precious little ring box, and there was a ceramic horse and carriage – minus the horse. It had long before been broken off. But it was pink and white and all glittery. I chose the carriage. For days, I worried that I had made the wrong choice.

Let's zip right along to 7th grade. I was a goofy, awkward young lady. Certainly not one of those in the popular group. But somehow I summoned the courage to try out for the school play. I don't remember a whole lot about the play, but the lead character's name was Flickie. We could choose which part we would audition for – and although I completely believed that Susan, the head cheerleader, was the only one who could possibly get the part, I still auditioned to be Flickie. I spent the next few days vacillating between fantasizing that I got the part, and berating myself for even trying.

I was in high school. My best friend, Sandy, didn't go to our school and wasn't even in our ward. But we got together often at stake events and at weekend parties. Sandy and I both liked Larry at the same time. I cried and cried trying to decide if my loyalty to Sandy was worth forgetting about flirting with Larry.

I was 18 years old and living on my own, but I came home for the summer. Back in those days, there were no cell phones. So at college we had an apartment phone. This semester, the phone was registered in my name. This meant I was responsible to collect the money from my roommates to help pay for it each month. That was in the day when it was so expensive to make long-distance phone calls that I only talked to my parents once a month. Well, my roommates ditched me that last month without paying their parts of the bill and I went home to my parents owing over $100. With an exhausted bank account, there was nothing I could do but ask my parents for help. I didn't want them to think I was irresponsible. And I didn't want to burden them. I stressed about that $100+ for days!

I was a young married and we were living in our first apartment. We were having guests over for the first time and I was preparing a Japanese meal for all 4 of us. My husband wanted me to wear a shirt he bought for me for our honeymoon and I wanted to wear something else. This became a point of contention for us – so much so that we burned the dinner and filled our house with smoke. Oh WHAT would we do when the guests arrived?!

I could go on, but we'll stop there. Just a quick re-cap: An infant being passed around to strangers, but Mom is within reach; choosing a trinket as a 6-year-old; auditioning for a school play; liking a boy who my best friend liked; money problems; wanting to impress friends. At the time, these things seemed monumental to me. I cried over each incident. I fretted over each thing. But as I retell them now – don't they seem a little silly? These might be things we can each consider "small stuff," right?

Now, a disclaimer: Small stuff is important to Heavenly Father! He wants us to talk with Him about it. BUT He doesn't want us to obsess about it. He hopes for us that we will approach Him in faith with all the "small stuff" and trust that He will help us, as He has promised.

1. Alma 34:20-26 "Cry unto him when ye are in your fields, yea, over all your flocks. Cry unto him in your houses, yea, over all your household, both morning, mid-day, and evening. Yea, cry unto him against the power of your enemies. Yea, cry unto him against the devil, who is the enemy to all righteousness. Cry unto him over the crops of your fields, that ye may prosper in them. Cry over the

flocks of your fields that they may increase. But this is not all; ye must pour out your souls in your closets, and your secret places, and in your wilderness..."

2. Matthew 6:25-34 "Therefore I say unto you, take no thought for your life, what ye shall eat, or what ye shall drink; nor yet for the body, what ye shall put on. Is not the life more than meat and the body more than raiment? Behold, the fowls of the air; for they sow not, neither do they reap, nor gather into barns; yet your Heavenly Father feedeth them. Are ye not much better than they? Which of you by taking thought can add one cubit to his stature? And why take ye thought for raiment? Consider the lilies of the field, how they grow; they toil not, neither do they spin: And yet I say unto you, that even Solomon in all his glory was not arrayed like one of these. Wherefore, if God so clothe the grass of the field, which to day is, and to morrow is cast into the oven, shall he not much more clothe you, O ye of little faith? Therefore take no thought, saying, What shall we eat? Or, What shall we drink? or, Wherewithal shall we be clothed? ... for your Heavenly Father knoweth that ye have need of all these things. But seek ye first the kingdom of God, and his righteousness; and all these things shall be added unto you. Take therefore no thought for the morrow; for the morrow shall take thought for the things of itself. Sufficient unto the day is the evil thereof."

So, in addition to praying for help regarding the "small stuff" in our lives, what else can we do to keep things manageable?

Clean out your mental closets. Have you ever had a stage in your life when you're a little messy when it comes to your clothing closet? Can you imagine pulling out clothes for the day, trying them on and being dissatisfied, so pulling out something else? And then on and on and on … outfit after outfit. And then you have to rush out the door so you're not late, but you can't stand a messy bedroom – so you cram everything back into the closet and push hard to get the door closed? Imagine this goes on day after day. In fact, it gets worse because you go on a shopping spree and buy a couple of pair of shoes and a sweater. There's no shelving space left in your closet, and the phone is ringing and someone is at the door – so you toss the 2 shoe boxes and the bag with your sweater into your closet, knowing you'll get to them later. Before you know it, clothes and shoes and purses and ties are piled knee high in the closet. Some clothes are barely hanging on to the hangers and in addition to the shoes you had (at one time) neatly arranged on the closet shelf, you've added books, Christmas presents, and yes … some of the clothes that you threw into the closet one of those mornings. You can't find a thing. You are afraid to even open the closet because everything will come bursting out. And in the morning when you think, "I have nothing to wear," that's not far off the mark – because you can't actually *find* anything.

Our minds can get cluttered and messy just like our clothing closets can. We have to keep our mental closets cleaned out if we want to learn to stop sweating the small stuff.

My college daughter called me not long ago, and rattled off a list of all the things that were stressing her at the moment. Mixed into that list were some urgent, really important things like getting her financial aid released to her so her rent could be

33

paid. She had till 5:00 that afternoon to take care of it. Also mixed into the list of stressors were less urgent, less important things. Stressors like overhearing that a friend had gossiped about her. The list was fairly long and clearly confusing. I gave her the advice that my parents had taught me: Clean out your mental closet. Grab a piece of paper and get it out of your mind and onto paper. The steps for cleaning out your mental closet are simple. And the effect is almost magical. By following these steps, it becomes easy to recognize what is small stuff and what is not. And it is also helpful in driving us to follow Eve's and Esther's examples in moving forward in faith.

1. **Identify the stressor.** I find it easier to really identify it when I force myself to write it down. Because of this, sometimes when I get ready to write it down, I realize it's not worth occupying the paper – or my mind. And I can just let it go. Otherwise, I identify it in a succinct way.

2. **One-by-one examine the following:**
   a. **Worst-case scenario:** What is the very worst thing that can happen in this situation I've just identified? Maybe it's small (I'll have to buy the cookies for the event rather than bake them) or maybe it's large (We'll lose our home and have to move in with our parents). Whatever it is, figure out what the very worst thing that could happen is. And then recognize that seldom the worst happens. But accept that it could. This step has actually taught me some important things about the difference between wants and needs. And it's been surprising to me, when I've completed this step, to recognize how truly freeing it is to accept certain losses – even before they happen. While

accepting this "worst-case scenario" I've been able to move forward to the next step.

b. **Steps to prevent it:** Now that you've identified and accepted the worst, plan the steps required to prevent it. Although you've found you can live with the worst, it's still not ideal. So prayerfully consider what you have control over and what you don't. List the things you can actually *do* to achieve a more desirable outcome.

c. **When to take those steps:** This is a planning time. If you're not already an organized person, this will help you incorporate that characteristic into your life. Make a time plan, and stick with it. Just knowing you have a plan to carry out these preventative steps will relieve a lot of stress.

d. **Shelve it.** Earlier I asked you to imagine a closet so cluttered and crammed full that you can't find a single thing in it. Now imagine an organized, beautiful closet with fewer items – all of them in their proper place. Clothing is hung neatly with space between the hangars. You've gotten rid of clothes that are just taking up space and this has made it possible for you to see what you actually have – clothes you choose to wear. On the floor are neatly placed shoes and on the shelf above the hanging clothes are carefully stacked labeled boxes. When you come home with something new, you know exactly where to place it. Our thoughts are like this. Now that you've identified, considered and accepted the worst thing that can happen, and planned your steps to get optimal outcome, place this situation that was previously a stressor neatly on your mental shelf, knowing you *will* pull it out and work on it according to the timeline you've planned.

Cleaning out our mental closets daily rather than waiting for them to get overwhelmed with stressors is a great preventive way of weeding out the "small stuff" and taking action with Heavenly Father guiding us on the things that are worthy of our attention.

1 Bad + 3 Good = Gratitude and No Sweat. We all have times when negative thoughts start to invade our minds, wreaking havoc on our attitudes and our actions. Negative thoughts, even though they may be based on a truth, actually qualify as "small stuff." There is nothing productive about negativity. Nothing. Negativity leads us down a dark alley and into a life of misery and lack of motivation. And so there is a remedy. If you're not a naturally optimistic person, follow this guideline: Allow yourself to have one negative thought. But you must stop there! Go ahead and think it, and then train your mind to think **3 good thoughts**. Give the three good thoughts at least as much time as you indulged in the negative thought. Make sure your 3 good thoughts are the last in your mind. Chances are that thinking those three good things will lead to a prayer of gratitude. When you're grateful, you don't sweat the small stuff. Your mind is too filled with gratitude to worry about anything at all! Remember, "And in nothing doth man offend God, or against none is his wrath kindled, save those who confess not his hand in all things, and obey not his commandments." (Doctrine & Covenants 59:21) When we are "sweating the small stuff" or surrounding ourselves with negative thoughts, there is no way that we are "confess[ing] his hand in all things." We're actually being pretty grumpy and feeling entitled – feeling that life isn't fair, that we're not being blessed. But if we allow ourselves only one negative thought to our three positive thoughts, we will better be able to see Heavenly Father's tender mercies in our lives. We will be able to view the difficulties for what they are: opportunities for growth. And we will stop sweating the small stuff.

Laugh. There is no better medicine than laughter. And this holds true when we want to kill off the disease of small-stuff-itis. If something is bothering you, laugh about it. For Harry Potter fans, this should be easy. Remember the spell, RIDDIKULUS? It's used against BOGGARTS. A boggart is the scariest things that one can imagine, and takes a different form for everyone. When the RIDDIKULUS charm is used against a Boggart, the scary creature is transformed into something so silly that you can't help but laugh. And it loses its ability to scare you.

Laughter is real magic. When something comes our way that is taking up our focus and creating negative energy inside of us, there is always a way to turn it into something hilarious. If it truly is "small stuff" then the only purpose it should serve in our lives is to make us laugh. If we identify a situation or a problem as being something that should not take up our time, one way to make it disappear is to find the humor in it. I guarantee there is humor – it may be well hidden, but if we look hard enough and allow our imaginations to run free, we will find it! And *POW* ... the previous boggart is just a joke.

Proper perspective. The last step for eliminating "small stuff" as stressors in our lives, allowing us to stop the sweating, is to gain proper perspective. We cannot see reality when we are living in a way that keeps the Spirit out of our lives. We end up with a skewed vision of what is right and what is wrong. We start to put importance on things that really don't matter. In short, we sweat the small stuff, thinking it's really important and deserves our focus. Following are three steps sure to align our perspective with honest reality:

1. **Righteous Living, otherwise known as Obedience to God.** President Thomas S. Monson said, "At times the wisdom of God appears as being foolish or just too difficult, but one of the greatest and most valuable lessons we can learn in mortality is that when God speaks and a man obeys, that man will always be right." *(Willing And Worthy To Serve, April 2012 General Conference)* When life starts to feel like it's controlling us, like everything is taking over our choices and we are spinning out of control, that's a sure sign that we're doing something that is not in harmony with Heavenly Father's guidelines. If, when everything seems to be going wrong, we take a moment to honestly examine our lives, we will clearly see what needs tweaking. We will recognize that there are good habits we have let slip, or attitudes that we've adopted that are not Christ-like. The world is no longer black & white. What was once considered right, is now the enemy to mainstream thinking. Everything turned gray, and now it's actually leaving gray-scale and getting reversed. "Woe unto them that call evil good, and good evil; that put darkness for light, and light for darkness; that put bitter for sweet, and sweet for bitter!" (Isaiah 5:20) When we are not obedient to God, our perspective becomes twisted and

we no longer know what is worth our time and what is not. Joseph Smith taught us, "Religion is not believing in the commandments only; it is in doing them." As we live the commandments that Heavenly Father has given us for our benefit, we are blessed with proper perspective.

2. **The Triple 7s:** Our family lived for a time in the Las Vegas area. Our stake president there was a man of great wisdom. He taught our youth what real 777 is. In the slot machines of Las Vegas when the 777 appears, you've hit the jackpot and bells go off, lights blink, and coins pour out of the machine. In the Henderson Lake Mead Stake, the youth were taught that 777 in their lives gives them the jackpot as well. 777 means that 7 days a week you say your morning prayers; 7 days a week you say your evening prayers; and 7 days a week you study your scriptures. And when you consistently complete your Triple 7s, the jackpot means regular guidance, direction, protection and always having the Spirit with you. My experience is that when I make a habit of scripture study and prayer, perspective is clear. When my perspective is clear, I am better able to dismiss the "small stuff" and put my focus on things that really matter.

3. **Serving Others.** When I let the "small stuff" get to me, I can be pretty sure that I'm focusing way too much on myself. My thoughts are of a selfish nature, and undoubtedly, my actions are also selfish. I've found that when I am being bothered by little things, if I consciously refocus my thinking on another person, the "small stuff" diminishes to its proper size and I can let go of it. When I go beyond thinking of another person to actually serving them in some way, my life is infused with energy

and hope. I see the world completely differently! All of a sudden, all the fuzziness in my life is lifted and I clearly see a beautiful existence. It's a simple thing, really, to think about another person. And when truly focusing on another, it's only natural to do something for him/her. Then it snowballs. My actions spur more appropriate thinking which spurs more action. And I'm blessed with a happier outlook and anticipation for what each moment will bring. That is when I stop focusing on little things that don't matter. I try each week to choose a person who will be the focus of my thoughts when I find I need to redirect. Then, as negativity or stress sneaks into my life, I quickly remember who I chose to think about. I find this is much easier – having a predetermined name of someone to focus my thoughts on – than trying to come up with someone while I'm self-absorbed. President Monson said, "Often small acts of service are all that is required to lift and bless another: a question concerning a person's family, quick words of encouragement, a sincere compliment, a small note of thanks, a brief telephone call. If we are observant and aware, and if we act on the promptings which come to us, we can accomplish much good." (Our Responsibility to Rescue, October 2013 General Conference) I believe the good we accomplish is not only beneficial for the person we serve, but also for ourselves.

In order to live in the moment, to really experience YOLO, we need to sweep away "small stuff" and fill our lives with things that matter. As Eve and Esther moved forward with their monumental decisions, putting their faith-filled thoughts into action, they provided for us great examples of focusing on the important as they didn't sweat the small stuff.

CHAPTER 3
URGENT vs IMPORTANT

Have you ever been forgotten? I mean – you're 8 years old and your mom forgets to pick you up from school … the teacher takes you to the office where you nervously wait for what feels like *days* till Mom finally arrives. My mom's best friend when I was 10-years-old was named Lorna. She'd open the door, holler "knock-knock," and my mom would call out "Come in Lorna!" Then they'd have a nice chat together. Well, I overheard Lorna tell my mom about the time she forgot her daughters. And it wasn't from school. They were on a family trip, minus Dad who couldn't make it, and this was in the 70s – way before cell phones. They were driving cross country and stopped for gas. Everyone climbed out to use the restroom, then piled back in and they took off. They were in an entirely different state when the Highway Patrol finally caught up to them. Not only that, the police didn't even have their daughters – they had to turn around and drive 4 hours back to retrieve them. ☺ To make the event even more humiliating, by the time Lorna got back to the gas station TV crews were there interviewing the girls. They'd had a grand time talking about how this is the sort of thing their mom does. So as a mom, I've been hyper-vigilant about never forgetting my children. And never being so late that they think they've been forgotten. I'm also a bit of a punctual addict. For me, 10-minutes early is "on time." My family and I lived in Henderson, NV – major desert. It gets ridiculously hot there during the summer. We actually moved there from a temperate rainforest where the average July temperature is 61 degrees. We left the cool, rainy weather to be welcomed to Las Vegas with triple digit heat that just sucked every ounce of moisture from us. But I digress. It was a typically hot July day a couple of years ago when I was rushing from location to location to make sure everyone was where they needed to be on time. I was due in a minute and a half to pick up my daughter from her friend's home where she'd spent the night. She had another engagement just a half hour later, and time was of the essence. As I drove at the edge of the speed limit (ok, maybe just beyond the edge) I passed a 30-something-year-old woman carrying a baby on her back and pushing a shopping cart filled with groceries. I realized she had to have already walked a good mile or so, if her shopping had been at the nearest store. I had the clear impression: "Stop and offer her a ride." Ummm ... "Ok," I thought, "let me think about it." And I kept driving. My urgent, pressing need was greater than this important prompting. I was absolutely certain that if Heavenly Father would just listen to me for a second, He'd see that it was more important for me to hurry and get my daughter, and then come back and pick up the mother and child – than to make Sierra worry because I was late. I prayed, "Please let the mother and baby not die in this heat. Please prompt them to sit down and rest till I get back! ... Please, please, please ... please see things my way." Well, I kept driving. For about 15 seconds. I flipped around, piled their groceries into my car, cranked up my a/c for them and took them home. A quick text to my daughter and she understood. As I pushed their filled cart to the back of my car I could hardly believe how hard this must have been for her. Just seconds out of my cool car, pushing that cart then unloading groceries and I was drenched in sweat. It was another lesson, piled on top of a lifetime of lessons, about the vital need to put important things ahead of the urgent.

Eve and Esther are both amazing examples of placing important things ahead of urgent. The very fact that each of them focused their efforts on securing life for others over their own personal comforts teaches us that. Sometimes, our choices can be as confusing as Eve's and Esther's must have seemed for them. Most likely none of us will be called upon to risk our lives for another. But aren't we sometimes confronted with choices between two seemingly equally important things? Differentiating between the urgent and important may not be as easy as it seems it should be.

There are so many layers to the lives of Martha and Mary that are recorded in the New Testament. I love knowing that Martha made sure all the mundane details were taken care of. And I love Martha for her humility. When the Lord taught her, "Martha, Martha, thou art careful and troubled about many things: But one thing is needful: and Mary hath chosen that good part, which shall not be taken away from her" (Luke 10:41-42), then she internalized His gentle chastisement. We know this because later, when her brother, Lazarus died, it was Martha who, when she heard that Jesus was coming, "went and met him ..." (John 11:20) And it was Martha who first expressed her deepest faith in Him. "... if thou hadst been here, my brother had not died. But I know, that even now, whatsoever thou wilt ask of God, God will give it thee." (John 11:21-22) Then, Martha's bold declaration, "... Yea, Lord: I believe that thou art the Christ, the Son of God, which should come into the world." (John 11:27) Martha gives me great hope. She teaches me that when my heart is in the right place, I can be taught. My weaknesses can be exposed to me, and I can be grateful that I then know what they are. And with intentional effort I can change, and my weaknesses can become my strengths. Martha teaches me that although it may be my tendency to spend my days on urgent things, I can change that and focus my attention on what is truly important.

Maybe Martha's sister, Mary, was just naturally inclined to set aside the urgent and be aware of the important. Or maybe Mary cultivated that gift before Martha did – maybe Mary had the same tendencies Martha did, but she worked on them at an earlier time in her life and learned how to choose "the better part." We don't know. But what we *do* know is that Mary not only sat at Jesus' feet and carefully listened while Martha was preparing the meal, but it was Mary who brought "an alabaster box of very precious ointment, and poured it on his head, as he sat at meat." (Matthew 26:7) Remember that His disciples criticized this? They thought it wasteful that this expensive ointment was being used in this manner. "When Jesus understood it, he said unto them, Why trouble ye the woman? For she hath wrought a good work upon me ... For in that she hath poured this ointment on my body, she did it for my burial." (Matthew 26:10,12) What an example Mary is for us! Certainly that family had living costs. I wonder if Mary had to wrestle with herself at all over the cost of the ointment. I don't know – but I know that she chose the better part at that time, too. She was clearly spiritually in-tune. She was guided and inspired. And she acted on that inspiration. Mary must have regularly chosen the important over the urgent – it seems that was part of who she really was. At some point, Mary learned to live that principle.

Are you a list maker? Can you relate to my quirky habit of writing parts of my daily list retroactively? That is – I do something – like, I don't know, brush my teeth – then hurry and write it on my list so I can cross it off. Yup – you know what I mean! If you keep lists – think back on your most recent list. What was on it? If you're like me, it's things like:

- Laundry
- Scrub the toilet
- Pay bills
- Buy paper towels

Some of you are probably better than this – some of you may add to that list things like:

- Scripture study
- Morning & evening prayers
- Home teaching

I'm a great believer in lists, so I don't want to discourage that activity. But think for a moment how different our days would be if our lists looked more like this:

- Recognize and act immediately on all promptings
- Prepare all day for tomorrow's temple visit
- Smile at everyone I see
- Focus today on what it means to be sanctified
- Find someone to serve
- Answer the phone when my sister calls.

I tried an experiment with a group once. They each received a candy kiss and were asked to open it and pop it in their mouths. Then just suck on it … don't bite, don't chew. When we discussed the experience, we began to talk about how it relates to life: Sometimes do we rush through everything as if it's a task? No matter how enjoyable it can be, we just bite into it and devour it – and then we move on to the next task, or the next prompting, or the next person needing us. What would happen if we stopped ourselves from biting and swallowing everything that comes our way each day and instead we savor it? Now, I'm not talking about savoring the gigantic Q-tip the doctor is using to gag you to see if you have strep. But I AM talking about savoring that phone call from your sister; savoring the walk to your next class; and maybe even forgetting you're trying to finish the chapter in 2nd Nephi and instead stopping at that Isaiah verse and finding a way to savor it.

"Some of us are so busy that we feel like a cart pulled by a dozen work animals – each straining in a different direction." *(Are You Sleeping Through the Restoration? Deiter F. Uchtdorf, April 2014 General Conference)* Do we find ourselves faced with conflicting priorities on a regular basis?

"When God comes first in our lives, whatever comes second will likely change tomorrow. Furthermore, whatever comes second for me will likely be different for you. When God comes first in our lives, however, whatever comes second will always be right. Like Mary, Hugh Nibley found that gospel study is especially powerful as a means to know what should come second on any given day. He observed that if you're not sure what you should be doing, read particularly the Book of Mormon. It is either the best thing you should be doing at the time or it will quickly put you on to what you should be doing." *(Mary, Martha, and Me: Seeking The One Thing That is Needful, Camille Fronk Olson)*

Can we set aside the urgent? Can we ignore it? Probably not. We're mortal which requires mortal tasks. We have to eat, we have to pay bills, we have to attend our classes if we hope to graduate. But can we *schedule* the urgent, leaving plenty of time for the important? Consider using a mobile device or even a calendar stuck on your fridge. There are lots of "urgent" things that really can be scheduled. Doctor visits, cleaning the house, car tune-ups, helping in the classroom … that sort of thing. Of course, last-minute emergencies will arise, but when we schedule what we can, we are then able to make room for the truly important things in our lives.

The previous chapter helped us evaluate what is urgent versus what is important. Often "small stuff" is urgent. Sometimes it doesn't even make it to the urgent level. But the "small stuff" *never* makes it to the important level. There are some things that should be classified as *important* for all of us. These include:

1. **Relationships.** "Thou shalt love the Lord thy God with all thy heart, and with all thy soul, and with all thy mind … Thou shalt love thy neighbor as thyself." (Matthew 22: 37, 39) These are the first and second great commandments. We know that all commandments are given for our benefit. These two – the greatest of all commandments – have to do with relationships. When we're talking about what is really important, where our efforts should be, our relationships rank right near the top of our "important lists."

2. **Testimony.** When we're scheduling our urgent and our important activities, growing our testimonies should definitely be high on our lists among the important. Heber C. Kimball said, "The time is coming when no man

49

or woman can endure on borrowed light. Each will have to be guided by the light within himself. If you do not have it, you will not stand." There are few things we take with us into the next life, and testimony is one of them. When we're working on our To Do Lists, including anything that builds testimony should make it on the list. In the October 2014 General Conference, Elder Neil A. Anderson said, "To the youth listening today or reading these words in the days ahead, I give a specific challenge: Gain a personal witness of the Prophet Joseph Smith … A testimony of the Prophet Joseph Smith can come differently to each of us. It may come as you kneel in prayer, asking God to confirm that he was a true prophet. It may come as you read the Prophet's account of the First Vision. A testimony may distill upon your soul as you read the Book of Mormon again and again. It may come as you bear your own testimony of the Prophet or as you stand in the temple and realize that through Joseph Smith the holy sealing power was restored to the earth … There will be family members and friends who will need your help. Now is the time…" Whether it's building our testimonies of Joseph Smith or of any other aspect of the gospel, it is worthy of our time.

3. **Progression.** Also in the October 2014 General Conference was a terrific talk by Elder Tad R. Callister. He said, "Pray for things of eternal consequence." All things of eternal consequence should make the list labeled *important*. With mortality being just a step in our eternal progression, certainly things that help us progress should make it to the *important* list as well. And so we should ask ourselves: Where am I headed? Do I know what my path is and what I want my future to be? There are specific helps in our lives to guide us.

a. **Divine Currents.** Elder Richard G. Scott taught us in the October 1999 General Conference, "The Lord has placed currents of divine influence in your life that will lead you along the individual plan He would have you fulfill here on earth. Seek through the Spirit to identify and carefully follow that direction that the Lord has put in your life. Align yourself with it. Choose, willingly, to exercise your agency to follow it. Do not be overcome by concentrating solely on today, its challenges, difficulties, and opportunities. Such preoccupations must not capture your attention so as to consume your life. Oh, how I would encourage you to weave deeply into the fabric of your soul the recognition that your life now is part of a much bigger plan the Lord has for you." It is through prayer and pondering combined with scripture study that we can recognize those currents of divine influence. Throughout the scriptures we are encouraged to pray always. As we turn constant prayer into a habit in our lives, we will be more able to recognize these currents of divine influence in our lives.

b. **Patriarchal Blessings.** Beyond looking to our Patriarchal Blessings as a personal guide to our progression, we would all be wise to follow the counsel offered by Elder Carlos A. Godoy in the October 2014 General Conference. "If you continue to live as you are living, will the blessings promised in your Patriarchal Blessing be fulfilled?" With this question in mind, we will make course corrections throughout our lives. And those changes will keep us on a path of progression.

c. **Turning Our Wills to Him.** If we truly hope to progress, to recognize important things that we should work on, we must be seeking after His will rather than going after our own agendas. "Rather than walking in their own way, true disciples walk in the path pointed out and prepared by their Master. Instead of creating God in their image, true Saints seek to be conformed to the image of Christ and to allow that image to shine in their countenances." *(Coming to Know Christ, Robert L. Millet)*

d. **Small Things of Great Importance.** Oftentimes, it is smaller things that can help us make the biggest leaps in our progression. That is, small things that make the *important* list. John Bytheway said, "The small and simple acts you make to put on the armor of God will bring about great things in your life." *(Armor Up!)* These small, important things can include:
   i. Prayer
   ii. Family Home Evening
   iii. Individual and Family Scripture Study
   iv. Sunday Meeting Attendance
   v. Temple Attendance
   vi. Fulfilling Our Callings.

Although we can, in a general sense, identify the important, it's my belief that what is truly important may vary among individuals. So how do I figure out *my* important things?

1. **What are my hopes and dreams?** In the October 1996 General Conference, Elder Neal A. Maxwell spoke about the desires of our hearts. He taught us, "Desire denotes a real longing or craving. Hence righteous desires are

much more than passive preferences or fleeting feelings... Whenever spiritually significant things are under way, righteous desires are present." We know that the Nephites were blessed with righteous desires when Christ visited them. "... they did not multiply many words, for it was given unto them what they should pray, and they were filled with desire." (3 Nephi 19:24) Righteous desires are given to us when we appropriately seek for them. When we are striving to live righteously, we can be sure that the hopes and dreams we have are worth pursuing. We can consider those hopes and desires as *important* on our lists.

2. **Take Inventory**. Where will I be 5 years from now? Does that fit in with my divine current? We need to constantly be evaluating ourselves, our lives, and the direction of our progression. Setting aside personal inventory time each week will serve us well.

3. **Adjust.** Some people question how they can feel good about going a certain direction in their lives only to have that direction change (*Was this really inspiration?*). But I've learned that just because something that I've put my effort into, feeling inspired, and then don't get the outcome I believe my efforts should lead to, doesn't mean that I wasn't inspired in the first place. It means that I put my effort in and that the outcome wasn't *my* will, but was *Heavenly Father's* will. It is an opportunity to not only grow faith, but also to prove my obedience. Sometimes, figuring out what is really important then having that change is a real test. But eventually it pays off. I had an experience that really hammered this point home and recorded it in my journal: Gaynor, a beautiful grandmother with a sweet South African accent, was scrolling through Facebook posts. Up popped my post: "Guess what? We're moving to Southeast Idaho! We're

thrilled, but will really miss our Henderson friends. Anyone have moving boxes you want to be rid of? Oh … and we're selling our house too. Any takers ☺ ?" Immediately my phone started beeping out of control with reactions to the news. One of the first was from Gaynor: "We'll miss you. My friends are looking for a house, not sure if they found one yet." 10-minutes later there was a BANG BANG BANG on the door. 70-something-year-old David had a sticky note in his hand with their home and cell phone numbers on it, just in case no one answered the door. "Gaynor told us you're selling your home. Have you listed it yet?" I invited David and Marceil into the house, not even realizing how sloppy my presentation was. I had spent the morning scrubbing every square inch of our kitchen with a magic eraser, turning it into a celestial, sparkling white. That was step 1 of the 3 things the realtor required before he would list the house next week. (Scrub everything till it shines, replace the carpet, touch up the walls.) So, although *I* was a mess, the kitchen was gorgeous. Brad had accepted the job in Idaho Falls a week earlier while I was in Texas; we met in Utah a couple of days after that for our friend's funeral, then drove home on Saturday with Azure and her friend in the back seat of the car. Brad set up a Monday night visit from the realtor. This was Tuesday morning. Everything was happening so fast – really, before we had a chance for the two of us to discuss much at all. As David and Marceil walked into our home, she gasped. Hands over her heart, she turned all the way around, pausing at the big picture of Christ as the Creator on our living room wall. "Beautiful, just beautiful! And look at how much light they have, David. It's just beautiful!" I invited them to walk through the house with me and told them that we would be replacing

54

the carpet. "Oh no! Don't do that. Don't do anything. We want to buy your house just as it is!" *What?!? They hadn't seen the missing sink handle, the hole in the screen door, all the flaws.* I started to feel giddy. And my arms erupted in goose-bumps. I looked at Marceil and she was wiping away tears. "This kitchen … it's so white! I always wanted a white kitchen, David." 5 minutes later, they had seen the house and the yard and we sat down in the living room. "We have been looking so hard. Praying even harder. We are exhausted. We have to be out of our home on Friday. Last night we looked at a house across the way … it was horrible. It was scary. There were things written on the walls I won't repeat. But it felt evil. To walk into a home with the Spirit being present, to feel good in your home, to know there's a chance it can be our home … what a miracle! Heavenly Father is so mindful of us!" *Mindful of **them**? It was clear to me that a miracle was unfolding in our lives … but this couple felt like it was **their** miracle.* It had been a couple of weeks filled with the Spirit for me. Marceil said she was exhausted. I felt the same. I'd experienced the unmatchable joy of being with all of my siblings and my parents for a few days; the heartbreak of losing Tiffany; the peace of Heavenly comfort; the security of reuniting with my husband and children; the excitement of positive change; the relief of upcoming stability … all over a period of just a few days. Yes. I was exhausted too. My spiritual experiences had been plentiful enough to fill a book. And now another … this one, an obvious miracle that could have only been divinely orchestrated. A miracle that had to be months, even years in the planning – that required the compliance of many people turning their will to Him and following guidance and inspiration. In my mind I pictured committees in Heaven, and the cheering as they pulled it all together and watched the result of all of their careful work. And the Spirit was SO strong in our home those moments. Angels were among us, their participation clearly sanctioned by Heavenly Father. Could Tiffany have gotten this rewarding first assignment, to help in some way? I don't know – but it felt like she was there. I had the thought: *It's so good that we didn't get an opportunity to move before this. It would have been so hard on Tiffany to have her last friends leave her.* The timing of all of this could not have been planned by mortals – too many people were affected by it. David and Marceil left with the promise to buy our home. Two days later we signed the papers, exactly a week after Brad and I met up in Utah for Tiffany's funeral. No carpet to replace, no agent fees to pay, no rush to leave before we're ready. And for David and Marceil, an address to forward their mail to; a safe environment to store their household treasures; and the peace of knowing they will be settled soon. Gaynor had opened her computer at the right time. And then she called David & Marceil. Did she know she was Heaven's Hands? How often, over the past 6 ½ years, have Brad and I hunted for jobs; worked in less-than-optimal conditions; "pushed against the rock" without it seeming to budge? My testimony of doing all we can, then accepting Heavenly Father's will with a happy heart, has solidified. I know that as we pray for direction and answers, then move forward resolutely, with an optimistic attitude, and in strength – in Heavenly Father's time, we are rewarded with what He knows is best for us. And when it is His time, committees of angels unite and mortals become the Hands of Heaven as He unfolds great miracles before our very eyes. I know He is mindful of every single one of His children. I know He can turn everything for our good, if we allow it. I know that great growth takes place through experience, adversity, and through humble acceptance of His will. These past two weeks I have felt as if I am the most blessed person on Earth. I have been carried and lifted, strengthened and rewarded. What a gift – to be a mortal and see Divinity at work!

The "pushing against the rock" story is one I've been familiar with for years. It is not credited to a particular author, but is so applicable to identifying the important things in our lives, adjusting as needed, and moving forward with faith. Here is the story:

There once was a man who was asleep one night in his cabin when suddenly his room filled with light and the Saviour appeared to him.

The Lord told him He had a work for him to do, and showed him a large rock explaining that he was to push against the rock with all his might. This the man did, and for many days he toiled from sunup to sundown; his shoulder set squarely against the cold massive surface of the rock, pushing with all his might. Each night the man returned to his cabin sore and worn out, feeling his whole day had been spent in vain.

Seeing that the man showed signs of discouragement, Satan decided to enter the picture - placing thoughts in the man's mind, such as ``Why kill yourself over this?, you're never going to move it!'' or ``Boy, you've been at it a long time and you haven't even scratched the surface!'' etc., giving the man the impression the task was impossible and the man was an unworthy servant because he wasn't moving the massive stone.

These thoughts discouraged and disheartened the man and he started to ease up in his efforts. ``Why kill myself?'' he thought. ``I'll just put in my time putting forth just the minimum of effort and that will be good enough.'' And this he did or at least planned on doing until, one day, he decided to take his troubles to the Lord.

``Lord,'' he said, ``I have labored hard and long in Your service, putting forth all my strength to do that which You have asked of me. Yet after all this time, I have not even budged that rock even half a millimeter. What is wrong? Why am I failing?''

To this the Lord responded compassionately, ``My friend, when long ago I asked you to serve Me and you accepted, I told you to push against the rock with all your strength and that you have done. But never once did I mention to you that I expected you to move it. At least not by yourself. Your task was to push. And now you come to Me, your strength spent, thinking that you have failed, ready to quit. But is this really so? Look at yourself. Your arms are strong and muscled; your back sinewed and brown. Your hands are calloused from constant pressure and your legs have become massive and hard. Through opposition you have grown much and your ability now far surpasses that which you used to have. Yet still, you haven't succeeded in moving the rock; and you come to Me now with a heavy heart and your strength spent. I, my friend will move the rock. Your calling was to be obedient and push, and to exercise your faith and trust in My wisdom, and this you have done.'' (Author Unknown)

As I contemplate making adjustments in where we focus our thoughts and efforts, I'm reminded of the beautiful verse in Ecclesiastes 3:1, "To every thing there is a season, and a time to every purpose under the heaven." What, at one time in our life may be just urgent, may at another time be truly important.

As we put forth effort to live YOLO, recognizing (as Eve and Esther did) the difference between things that are urgent and those that are important, President Gordon B. Hinckley's statement is certainly applicable: " ... take stock of yourselves ... Pray for guidance, for help, for direction, and then follow the whisperings of the Spirit to guide you in the most serious of all responsibilities ..." *(Each a Better Person, October 2002 General Conference)*

CHAPTER 4
OPENING THE DOOR FOR CHRIST

Once Adam and Eve left the Garden of Eden, mortality took over – life got hard. No longer walking and talking with God, they still needed guidance. Just because they were no longer in the Garden didn't mean that God had left them. It didn't mean they were alone. Heavenly Father and Jesus Christ continued to be available to Adam and Eve. But now, as mortals, Adam and Eve had to "open the door" and invite Deity into their lives.

The familiar picture of Christ standing at the door and knocking is a good visual for the way things really are. There is no handle on the outside of the door. Christ is there, waiting for us to open the door from the inside and welcome Him in.

When Esther was presented with an incredibly hard decision, her first course of action was to ask for Divine help. Knowing that the situation was grave, beyond her own abilities to handle, she invited many to join her in "opening the door" for Christ to direct her. I wonder how things may have been different if Esther was not a woman of faith. Or if Esther would have been proud and cocky rather than humble and submissive.

We all must humbly keep our doors propped open with a warm invitation for Christ to enter our lives.

I grew up in a family of six siblings. I had a brother just older than me – one grade ahead of me in school - and a brother only 15 months younger than me. My older brother, Bruce, was everything a high school boy wants to be: football star, class president, good-looking, popular with everyone. I was known by teachers and peers as "Bruce's little sister." He was way too cool to associate with me. In fact, sometimes I even felt sorry for him – that people had to know he was related to me. But most of the time I just felt sorry for myself. How I longed to be liked by Bruce and his friends! Bruce had a busy life with practices after school and social events after that. Even if he had wanted to include me, he probably wouldn't have had time. But I saw it all as rejection. I just knew he despised me and wished he didn't know me. I avoided him in the hallways so I wouldn't feel bad if he didn't say hi. I honestly thought he hated me. My life changed one night. Dad took us to Mutual where we met with our separate classes. Afterwards, while waiting for rides, one boy my age grabbed my sweater from me. As I was trying to get it back, he threw it on the ground and started to run away. He ran right smack into my big brother. Bruce grabbed him by the shirt collar, demanded he pick up the sweater, and growled to him, "That is my *sister*. Don't you *ever* treat her like that again!" In that one moment my self-worth changed. He had acknowledged me as his sister. He was protective of me and proud of me. From that moment on, though teachers and friends saw Bruce as a football star or class president, to me he was my protector, my tender-hearted brother. I started to "open the door" for Bruce, inviting him into my life rather than assuming he wanted nothing to do with me. The next year I had gained enough self-esteem to run for class president myself! Bruce helped with my campaign and cheered at my speech. Given his position as Senior Class President, he was present for the counting of the ballots. When it was all over and he pulled me aside to tell me I had lost, I hardly felt sad at all. Because in telling me he also said, "I couldn't cheat for you, but I did cheer for you ... every time a vote came in for you, I cheered." I felt like a winner for months after that. I realized my brother had been there for me all along – he wasn't the distant, unaware person I thought he was. I just needed to recognize him as my brother and invite him into my life.

Christ is our brother. He is there – knocking at the door, waiting to be invited in. When I thinking about "inviting" there is a feeling of personal warmth associated with it. As we invite, we really are welcoming someone into either our personal space or to a special event. We invite to parties, to dinner, to weddings, to visits. Always, when we invite, we make preparations to welcome the attendees. Some of those preparations could include cleaning our home, planning activities or preparing food. This can be time consuming and sometimes even exhausting. But almost always it is exciting and energizing as we mentally prepare for those we invite to attend. Have you ever extended a last-minute invitation and been *so glad* that your house was already clean? Or that cookies were in the cookie jar? Or that the feeling in your home was happy and comfortable without having to hurry and make last-minute preparations?

When we invite Christ in through our personal doors, have we spent time so we are adequately prepared without having to rush to get things ready? I'm reminded of the parable of the 10 Virgins. All ten of them had good intentions and righteous desires. They all hoped for the same outcome. Yet some were prepared and some were not. Some were ready without having to scramble at the last minute. Some were blessed with His presence, and others missed out. Are we taking steps to keep our lamps always filled so we are ready? Christ is *always* at our door. Are we always ready to open it?

Preparations to open the door and welcome Christ into our lives are similar to preparing our home for guests.

- **Clean.** When inviting important guests into our home, all of us would not only tidy up the clutter, but we would also scrub the floors, do the dishes, clean the windows. We'd pay attention to the details. And so it is when we invite Christ into our lives. We must be clean. This means obedience. It means consistent repentance. "No matter what your current status, the very moment you voluntarily choose honest, joyful, daily repentance by striving to simply do and be your very best, the Savior's Atonement envelops and follows you, as it were, wherever you go. Living in this manner, you can truly 'always retain a remission of your sins' (Mosiah 4:12) every hour of every day, every second of every minute, and thus be fully clean and acceptable before God *all the time.*" *(Approaching the Throne of God With Confidence, Elder Jorg Klebingat, October 2014 General Conference)* Being clean means retaining remission of our sins. But what does *remission* mean? When we think about the word remission in relation to diseases of the body, we realize that dismissal of the disease may be temporary. It could come back. But King Benjamin made it clear that we can *always retain a remission* of our sins! Imagine always being able to retain remission of a disease. I'm sure that wouldn't come without hard work. Even so, always retaining a remission of our sins takes concentrated, consistent, hard work. And just as a house doesn't just "stay clean," we don't become clean one time (as in baptism) and that's it. We continually repent and work hard so that through the Atonement we can be cleansed constantly.

- **Offerings.** Just as we serve refreshments – something we offer to our guests when we invite them in, we must always be prepared with offerings when inviting Christ into our lives.
    - **Broken heart and contrite spirit.** If we really want Christ near us, we will offer him our broken heart and contrite spirit! "The Lord is nigh unto them that are of a broken heart; and saveth such as be of a contrite spirit." (Psalm 34:18) Elder Gerald N. Lund spoke in the April 2008 General Conference of this. "... carefully assessing the condition of our hearts is one of the most essential things we can do in this life." (*Opening Our Hearts, April 2008*) Why is this? The truth is that our actions may be ok, but if our hearts are not in the right place, there is no growth, there is no humility, and there is no reliance on the Savior. Opening the door to the Lord consists of opening our hearts. A heart that is whole and not broken is a closed heart. It is not open. "When our hearts are broken, we are completely open to the Spirit of God and recognize our dependence on Him for all that we have and all that we are. The sacrifice so entailed is a sacrifice of pride in all its forms. Like malleable clay in the hands of a skilled potter, the brokenhearted can be molded and shaped in the hands of the Master." (*Elder Bruce D. Porter, "A Broken Heart and a Contrite Spirit, October 2007 General Conference)* As our hearts break, they prepare our spirits to be contrite. When we

have this offering firmly in place, our invitation to Christ to enter our lives is successful.

- o **Remembering the Sacrament Prayers.** How loving and mindful the Lord is of us that He gives us a weekly opportunity to remember and to recommit! Not only partaking of the sacrament, but also remembering the prayers throughout the week is an offering that is acceptable to the Lord. Remember, we promise that we are willing. This infers that we humbly give our will to Him. We are willing to take His name! "In as many ways as possible we try to take upon us His identity, and we begin by taking upon us His name. That name is formally bestowed by covenant in the saving ordinances of the gospel. These start with baptism and conclude with temple covenants, with many others, such as partaking of the sacrament, placed throughout our lives as additional blessings and reminders." (*Elder Jeffrey R. Holland, April 2006 General Conference*) Taking His name is a serious matter. This means we are willing to be a representative of Him, and it gives meaning to the phrase, "every member a missionary." Like it or not, our words and our actions are proselyting either for the Lord or for the adversary. When we remember, daily, that we have promised to willfully take His name, we are more cautious in what we say and do. And He draws near to us. In the same thought, we promise to always remember. As with all commandments and covenants, they are gifts to

66

us, to provide joy in this life and to guide us back to His presence. When we remember, our doors open wider and He can enter. We also commit to keep His commandments. Keeping His commandments provides us with a clear conscience and the confidence to invite Him in.

- o **We Love.** "Above all else, loving with 'the pure love of Christ,' that gift that 'never faileth,' that gift that 'beareth all things, believeth all things, hopeth all things, [and] endureth all things.' Soon with that kind of love, we realize our days hold scores of thoroughfares leading to the Master and that every time we reach out, however feebly, for Him, we discover He has been anxiously trying to reach us." (*Elder Jeffrey R. Holland, April 2006 General Conference*) Charity, or in other words, loving as He does, is an offering that He accepts. Anyone with children knows that if someone wants to get on your good side, all they need to do is do something nice for your children. It warms our hearts and endears that person to us forever! And so, when we truly love another, it stands to reason that it warms our Heavenly Parents. Just as important, when we truly love another, our hearts are softened and we are open to feeling Christ near.

After opening the door, how, exactly, do we invite Christ in?

Incomprehensible to me is the fact that I am no longer a child in my parents' home. I have grown up! And in fact, *my* children have also grown up! For years it felt like I was just pretending

– like I had as a child when I would "play house." But as strange as it seems, I have grown up and left home, and our children have done the same. And so, when we are reunited for any length of time, it is joyful beyond description. Not long ago we welcomed all of our children home at the same time. We climbed onto a king-sized bed and talked and talked and talked. I would have loved to have frozen that moment, lived it forever! Even more recently my siblings and I all gathered at our parents' home. It was a similar experience. Our spouses and children weren't with us, so for a few short days it was like going back in time. We spent hours around the game table, usually erupting in laughter that actually hurt these soft bellies we've grown. Meeting up with friends is also joyful. It feels good to be with people who love me, accept me, and really know me.

As we think of our family and friends, we remember the happy times. But true to mortality, sometimes our friends may let us down. It is the way of life. But when we make the Savior our very best friend, remember He is also our brother, it gives new meaning to the word "friendship." What would it mean for our relationship with the Savior if we really made Him our best friend? Have you ever wondered *who in the world could possibly understand? Who will listen without judging? Who can I share this with and come away feeling* better *rather than worse?* When I was in the third grade I desperately wanted to be friends with the prettiest girl in school: Anna Marie Jenkins. She had pierced ears and long dark eyelashes. Everyone wanted to be her friend. One day during recess I plucked up the courage to go and talk to her. As I approached, even though she smiled at me, everyone else started whispering and giggling. I was awkward, but not deaf. I heard the mean things they were saying about me and I ran off to the far corner of the playground. Sitting in the dust against the chain link fence, bitter tears fell down my cheeks. I was hurt, discouraged, and absorbed in self-pity. Being just a few months shy of my 8th birthday, I had been thinking a lot about baptism. I was aware, even at that young age, of the commitment I would be making and of the personal relationship I had with Jesus. Suddenly, alone on the playground, I didn't feel so all alone. I remembered learning that when Jesus suffered for each of us in the Garden of Gethsemane, He suffered for all of our pains. I realized that the pain I was feeling right at that moment – He had already felt. And He had felt it for *me!* I dried my tears and got up and played. My heart was healed. I wasn't just acting the part of a happy child – I was truly happy, knowing that the price Jesus paid may have been a big price, but He did it because He loves me. That was a turning point in my life. I continued to be awkward, I continued to struggle at recess. But I never again felt alone. Without being able to articulate it, I knew that if Jesus had already paid the price, that *huge* price, I would be truly ungrateful if I didn't accept it. Inviting and welcoming Christ into our lives means seeing Him as our Friend. "Cry unto God for all thy support; yea, let all thy doings be unto the Lord, and whithersoever thou goest let it be in the Lord; yea, let all thy thoughts be directed unto the Lord; yea, let the affections of thy heart be placed upon the Lord forever." (Alma 37:36) He draws near to us, as we invite Him in by recognizing that He truly is our Best Friend.

What about listening? A friendship goes two ways. Yes, He wants to hear us. He wants us to tell him our joys and our sorrows. But if we never stop to listen, can it be a real friendship? If we just talk and don't actually listen, is the door really open? How does the Lord talk to us, and how do we know it's Him? Elder Richard G. Scott taught us in his April 2012 General Conference address, *How to Obtain Revelation and Inspiration For Your Personal Life*, "Two indicators that a feeling or prompting comes from God are that it produces peace in your heart and a quiet, warm feeling." Remember that when Oliver Cowdery was seeking confirmation that he was being instructed of the Lord, these words were given to him: "Did I not speak peace to your mind concerning the matter? What greater witness can you have than from God?" (Doctrine and Covenants 6:23) My husband and I were preparing to make a move. Actually, he had already left to begin his job in the new state while I stayed behind with our daughter for a few weeks until her graduation. And so our house shopping became a long-distance effort. We searched together on the internet – he in Idaho, me in Nevada – both on speaker phone as we looked at listing after listing. Hour after hour we searched, and finally narrowed it down to a dozen or so homes. Our real estate agent was completely accommodating and non-judgmental when we contacted her once again, saying that we felt an urgency. Could she show us the list of homes, in the order we've listed them? Oh – and all in one afternoon, please! Our agent went to work and set up the showings. The next day, after prayer that we would be guided and know which home was intended to be ours, I sat at the computer in Nevada while Brad and our agent visited the homes. Grateful for modern technology that allowed me to see what they were seeing – as long as Brad had the phone pointed in the right direction – we looked at each home starting at the beginning of our list. We both noted the things we liked, and what we could do to make each home work for us. When they would get in the car to go to the next home, I'd either cross that one off our list, or make notes next to it. One heart if it was nice, two if we loved it. It was the seventh house, one that we both thought was pretty, but we weren't thrilled with the location. They got out of the car and as they walked up the steps to the brick house, I felt it! *I love this house!* We weren't even inside yet. The walk through the house was quick, but everything I saw got me more and more excited. Brad liked it too, but I *loved it*. As they were preparing to leave the house, I told them that I just knew this was the one. I couldn't think of any reason to look at any more homes. I felt that peace, that warmth, that excitement! This was the one. But one of my requests when we first connected with our agent was that we try to find a home with fruit trees. This didn't have any. She had one more on our list that had lots of them. So we went ahead and checked out one more house. Nice. But not right. Late that night, after much discussion on the phone between my husband and myself, and much prayer, we asked the agent to make an offer on the house for us. As she was sending in the offer first thing the next morning, there was a glitch. She called the selling agent and found that the house had been sold. *How could this be? How could I feel that peace and know it was ours, but it was already sold?* I've had enough experience in my life to know that guidance and inspiration lead me to action. Those actions don't always end with the result I expect, but often lead me to other actions. And so, although disappointed, I knew I needed to pull up my bootstraps and move forward. I asked our agent to look for other houses in that area – on that street, in fact. Maybe it was the area, not the house, that we were feeling inspired about. Together we searched, me from my computer in Nevada, our agent from hers in Idaho. I kept Brad in the loop through text messages while he was at work. We set up some appointments for that evening and Brad even drove past one of the houses they would look at so he could check out the area. At noon our agent called me. "The selling agent for the house you love just called. The house hadn't actually sold. An offer had been given, the seller countered, and it's in limbo right now. We have a small window of opportunity. Should we make an offer?" It was just an hour later when my daughter and I were on our way to the grocery store. My phone beeped and Azure read the text to me: *The seller is going to sign your offer! That house was meant to be yours!* Of course we erupted in screams. I had heard Him. I knew that was our place. Or at least, I knew that He wanted me to *feel* that it was our place. The results were in His hands, but I had heard Him, and I had recognized His voice in my heart and in my mind. That's how we know it's Him that we hear. It *feels* right. It feels warm. It feels peaceful and good.

Our 18-year-old daughter was watching General Conference on the TV in her apartment in Rexburg on the day the age change for missionaries was announced. Just seconds after President Monson announced that young women could serve beginning at age 19, we were on the phone with Sierra. She had always planned on serving a mission, but was blindsided by the announcement. Although she had attended our stake's weekly Preach My Gospel missionary preparation classes for two years, she hadn't prepared financially or mentally to serve a mission within the next few months. And so when we were on the phone asking her if she was going to start her paperwork, she just didn't know. She told us she would pray about it and then we'd talk. Just an hour or so later, she called. "I knelt down to pray," she said. "But before I even began I knew. I had already felt it in my heart and in my mind. And the thought came to me – *Why are you asking if I've already told you?* I called the executive secretary and I have my first interview with the bishop this Tuesday!" Sierra had already felt His answer. And so, when she knelt in prayer a couple of years later to ask if the man she loves is the one she should marry, she remembered that General Conference Saturday. She knew. He had already spoken to her with peace and with warmth.

Opening the door for Christ and inviting Him into our lives is a daily process. It is a habit. And when it becomes comfortable, when it becomes familiar, we are more able to live each moment in joy *and* in peace. YOLO means making the most of each moment. And each moment is wonderful – no matter how hard it may be – when Christ is by our side!

CHAPTER 5
BECOMING

Remember when Alice, the Alice-in-Wonderland Alice, wakes up in her wonderland? She says, "I wonder if I've been changed in the night? Let me think ... was I the same when I got up this morning? I almost think I can remember feeling a little different. But if I'm not the same, the next question is: Who in the world am I? Ah ... that's the great puzzle!"

And so begins Alice's adventure through her wonderland. She explores and makes friends; takes some interesting turns and some wrong turns; but in the end, Alice returns home. Along the way she meets up with Caterpillar. Remember, the Caterpillar asks Alice, "Who ARE you?" And then, perhaps the most confusing conversation in Disney movies *ever* takes place! "I hardly know sir! I've changed so much since this morning, you see" ... "I do NOT C" and on and on. I love the Caterpillar because he makes Alice think. He isn't going to tell her who she is - he's going to make her discover it for herself.

And so must we all do. We are in a constant state of change, all of us. We are in the process of **becoming**.

I imagine the Caterpillar, who - in the Disney version, just disappears - actually "becoming" himself. He is also in a state of change. He is becoming a butterfly. But it's certainly not without effort. And it is not pain free. In fact, at the very time he thinks his life is ending, everything is actually coming together, and the caterpillar is changing into a butterfly. I love the quote, "When things seem like they're falling apart, in reality, they're usually falling into place."

Just like the caterpillar who is not only content as a caterpillar, but is probably actually contributing to society in a meaningful way and believes he is fulfilling his destiny and reaching his potential as a caterpillar, sometimes, we might be content as we are. Sometimes, we forget to continue to "become" .. when what Heavenly Father has in store for us is as spectacular a change as a butterfly is from a caterpillar!

It's easy to see how Eve is a model example of becoming. The choice she made to partake of the forbidden fruit in the Garden of Eden would cause more change than we can imagine. Her choice was essential for her personal quest to become her very best self. But it was more than that. Her choice was essential for the potential for *all of us* to "become." Eve's decision wasn't a flippant move. She put in time and effort, discussion and prayer, pondering and studying. What an example for all of us as we make our choices regarding the direction we are headed in order to become what Heavenly Father desires us to be.

Esther was thrown into her magical change from Jewish maiden to Queen. But Esther, just like Eve, provides a good example for us all. Although we are provided with very few details in the Bible, we can make some pretty good assumptions. First, she was kind and filled with charity. Esther "obtained favour in the sight of all them that looked upon her." (Esther 2:15) Physically beautiful women are popular to a point. But looks don't buy friendship. They don't create real relationships. Clearly Esther was beautiful. But beyond that, she was placed in a stressful situation — a life-changing position. And she chose to be kind, to work hard, and to make friends. She must have reached out to others to help them along the way. How else could she have obtained favor in their sight? As Esther moved toward becoming the Queen, she also sharpened her reasoning skills. With the help of Heaven she created a plan to save her people. Esther exercised great patience and great confidence as she exposed Haman, and his evil plans, to the king. In Esther's experience of becoming the person who would save her people, she never forgot who she was. She was humble, while taking courageous steps into the unknown. A fine example for us all as we, ourselves, work toward becoming.

We talked in an earlier chapter about list making. Lists are a great way to keep us moving forward. On a recent visit with my parents, my mother shared with me about a time in her life when everything on her *To Do List* started with a *To Become* phrase. For example: *Go To Walmart* changed to *I am becoming a great visiting teacher and serving others by going to Walmart to pick up a chocolate heart to give with the message*. Or here's another example: What normally would have been *Exercise* could be *I am becoming a more grateful recipient of the Atonement because I'm taking care of my body by exercising today.* See? A great practice is to take your To Do List for today, and turn each of the items into a To Become Statement.

This is one way we can recognize our worth today. We can clearly see that changing diapers and scrubbing floors are helping us to become. It is also a way to help us keep our eye on who *Heavenly Father* knows we are … we will accept and love the caterpillar we are – not because we are content to be a caterpillar, but because we know that our actions are leading us to become an amazing butterfly that takes flight and soars. Isn't it an interesting way of thinking? For those who don't understand that we are each divine, and that we are queens and kings in the making, the ego takes over - and at the same moment that we demean ourselves and think we're useless, we also start to think we're better than the lady at the airport cleaning toilets. Or we think that the hundreds of "likes" on our post exalts us. But for those who *do* understand our divine nature, or at least have a testimony of it ... we know that we are of infinite value. We know that who we are becoming brings glory to Heavenly Father and that we, all of us on this Earth, are equally loved and valued. We know there is something to be gained by association with the PTA president as well as the Taco Bell cashier. When we know that we are butterflies-in-the-making, we stop comparing and noticing injustices and competing. That is when we lift others as we lift ourselves, recognizing that every little mundane thing we do in this life can help us to *become.*

I've always loved prisms. They catch the light and create so much magical-looking beauty that they are just fun to look at! In the Las Vegas Temple Celestial Room there are two big chandeliers. Whenever I'm in the Celestial Room, I take notice of not just the magnificent chandeliers, but I also look around the room to see the beautiful patterns of light that the prisms in the chandeliers are reflecting. Not long ago I was at the temple at a time of day that I don't usually go. When I walked into the Celestial Room I was absolutely delighted to see reflections of the prisms creating flowers of light onto the floor! It was so pretty and so happy and so magical that I wanted to dance around and chase them. (That would have been inappropriate. ☺) But I thought, as I followed the reflections, about the prisms in those chandeliers always being there. Every single time I go to the temple, the prisms are there, where they belong, and are reflecting the light. But when I walk into the room, if it's even a minute later than it was the last time I was there, the light hits them a little bit differently and the reflection is a new pattern. It is the *light* that determines the reflective pattern, not the prism. If we become prisms, always facing the Savior, focusing our *To Become Lists* on Him, we will always be reflecting His light. And when we are facing Him, and truly giving our will to Him, He will move the light so it reflects in the way He desires. It's not our job to choose where, or which pattern the light reflects. It's our job to be a prism, open to His light, and to allow Him to use us to reflect according to His desire. When we do that, we are truly *becoming*.

What I love about that is it places *only proper responsibility* on us. It takes the ego out of the equation and allows us to humbly, and fully rely upon Him. It doesn't take our agency away, and it doesn't take away the pain and the work. If all the pain and challenges were gone, we'd simply be lumps of coal – and light doesn't reflect off of coal. We have to have our challenges in order to be prisms. They refine us so we can reflect His light.

I used to think that I could control everything. I really did! I thought that if I focused hard enough, thought hard enough and worked hard enough, I could always get the outcome I desired. That is both arrogant and scary. Isn't it so much more joyful, more peaceful, and actually more correct to work hard, pray hard, exercise faith *all the while, from the depths of our souls, desiring God's will*? I testify that it is.

Elder Neal A. Maxwell said, "Therefore, what we insistently desire, over time, is what we will eventually become and what we will receive in eternity." *(According to the Desire of Our Hearts, October 1996 General Conference)*

So, like Alice in her wonderland, our life is an adventure. And we get to choose! We'll make friends, we'll make mistakes. We'll try one path then decide another is better. Some days we'll wake up feeling changed; some days we'll wonder who we really are; sometimes we'll be enlightened by others on our paths, who will help us figure out who we really are and where we are going. After all, every one of us is here to help each other. But all of us, if we truly desire it, will wake up ourselves. Having had a great adventure and having learned and grown and *become*.

And if we are, all of us, in the process of *becoming*, this means that each of us on this Earth is in a constant state of change. With that being the case, isn't it best if we overlook the faults that may glare at us from another individual? Who knows what stage of *becoming* that person is in? We certainly don't! He may not know himself! Hanging on to past grudges, judging another by previously performed wrongs, labeling a person by who *we think* they are ... all of that is not only damaging to relationships, but it is negative thinking that takes up precious moments of our lives. Eleanor Roosevelt said, "Great minds discuss ideas; Average minds discuss events; Small minds discuss people." When we live our lives with the motto YOLO, we should certainly keep in mind our choices exercised in regards to what we choose to think and discuss. There is no place for gossipy, negative thinking or speaking for those who are working on *becoming*.

I remember having an internal conversation regarding someone whose words and actions had hurt me. It was on a Sunday after my daughter, Azure, pointed out the words to a beautiful hymn to me:

Should you feel inclined to censure
Faults you may in others view,
Ask your own heart, ere you venture,
If you have not failings, too.

Let not friendly vows be broken;
Rather strive a friend to gain.
Many words in anger spoken
Find their passage home again.

Do not, then, in idle pleasure
Trifle with a brother's fame;
Guard it as a valued treasure,
Sacred as your own good name.

Do not form opinions blindly;
Hastiness to trouble tends;
Those of whom we thought unkindly
Oft become our warmest friends.

(LDS Hymn Book #235, Should You Feel Inclined to Censure)

Pondering on my previous thoughts, I remembered something my dad has often said, "Assume that everyone is doing the best they can." Good advice! When that assumption is made, a sense of charity replaces condemnation. The hymns, as the scriptures, are filled with words of wisdom and great counsel. The hymn, *Truth Reflects Upon Our Senses* is another that always causes me introspection:

Truth reflects upon our senses;
Gospel light reveals to some.
If there still should be offenses,

Woe to them by whom they come!
Judge not, that ye be not judged,
Was the counsel Jesus gave;
Measure given, large or grudged,
Just the same you must receive.

Jesus said: "Be meek and lowly,"
For 'tis high to be a judge;
If I would be pure and holy,
I must love without a grudge.
It requires a constant labor –
All his precepts to obey.
If I truly love my neighbor,
I am in the narrow way.

Once I said unto another,
"In thine eye there is a mote;
If thou art a friend, a brother,
Hold, and let me pull it out."
But I could not see it fairly,
For my sight was very dim.
When I came to search more clearly,
In mine eye there was a beam.

If I love my brother dearer,
And his mote I would erase,
Then the light should shine the clearer,
For the eye's a tender place.
Others I have oft reproved,
For an object like a mote.
Now I wish this beam removed,
Oh, that tears would wash it out!

Charity and love are healing;
These will give the clearest sight;
When I saw my brother's failing,
I was not exactly right.
Now I'll take no further trouble;
Jesus' love is all my theme;
Little motes are but a bubble
When I think upon the beam.

Blessed Savior, thou wilt guide us,
Till we reach that blissful shore
Where the angels wait to join us
In thy praise forevermore.

(LDS Hymnbook #273, Truth Reflects Upon Our Senses)

While we are working on our own journey of *becoming*, it is safe to assume that everyone around us is doing the same. It's not an easy process – mortal life. We make many mistakes along the way. Our job is to pick ourselves up, determine to do better, then try harder. We have no business using precious moments of our time telling someone else what they should be doing on their journeys of *becoming*. We have no business even thinking about it! And, as mentioned earlier, when we do use our time that way, it is a terrible waste of precious moments. With mortality being a gift to us, I believe we will account for the moments we have been given. Won't it be wonderful, during that accounting, to share the progress we made – rather than report that we used those moments to berate others?!

It's easiest for me to let go of past hurts, to see people in a charitable way, and to guard my tongue when I take a moment to look at my own life. I am trying, every day, to be better. If I were judged today by others, according to who I was 10 years ago, it would be devastating! I have worked hard to be better and 10 years really has made a difference. Even if I were judged by who I was one week ago, it would not seem fair. So keeping in mind that I hope to be viewed according to who I am trying to be today, isn't it only right that I recognize that others, too, are in a constant state of change? And that they are "doing the best they can"?

The art of *becoming* is really the purpose of life. We were placed on this Earth to learn, to grow, to *become* like our Heavenly Parents. Like Alice in her Wonderland, it will be confusing at times. We may lose our way, we may become distracted. But it will be a great adventure if we choose so. We meet others along our journeys who are also trying to get home.

While working on becoming, we must remember who we really are. This short fairy tale illustrates how easy it is to forget:

> *Once upon a time, in a faraway kingdom lived some young princesses. They were not orphaned, and had no wicked step mother to boss them around. In fact, although their lives were sometimes hard, they had all they needed for a life of comfort. They had beds to sleep on, cell phones to text from, and delicious food to eat every single day. Sometimes the princesses would forget how well taken care of they were. In their minds they spent the day scrubbing floors, tending siblings, and doing homework. On the days they focused only on themselves, they often felt enslaved, as if they really did have a wicked step mother.*

One day a declaration was circulated throughout the kingdom inviting all the princesses near and far to come for a celebration. As I mentioned before, our little princesses had no wicked stepmother to lock them in the tower - there was no one and nothing preventing them from attending the celebration. But they had forgotten who they really were. They were so focused on what wasn't fair in their lives. Things like: a teacher cheating them out of a good grade; a friend spreading rumors about them; a sibling blaming them and their parents believing it; not being asked to homecoming; being asked by the wrong prince to homecoming; not making the team; getting sick. And it's true! Life for these princesses wasn't fair! But because they spent so much time thinking about what wasn't fair, these little princesses truly forgot that they were princesses. And when the declaration went out about the celebration - they thought they weren't invited. They knew that Princess Jessica was invited because she did everything right. They knew Princess Rachel was invited - she was so nice to everyone and never got angry. They knew Princess Amber would be going - she was beautiful and kind, and oh-so-talented! But because they had focused so much on themselves - on what wasn't going right, on how hard life was, and mostly how life just wasn't fair - they could no longer remember to put the "princess" at the front of their names. As they heard the declaration shouted by the Town Cryer, they thought, "Oh, won't that be lovely for the princesses? Life is so unfair. It's always the princesses who get everything. So while the princesses are out celebrating I'll just sit here with my phone and text my friends about how life stinks. And I'll get on Facebook and see how much fun all the princesses are having and maybe I'll even post a status that shows everyone how little I care. What-ev."

And so the princesses wasted away their days before the celebration. Instead of excitedly preparing, they focused even harder on what a sad life they'd been given. And the whole world seemed to get darker and darker until finally, the celebration day arrived. Our princesses did just as planned. They pulled out their phones and their laptops, slouched on the couch and melted into texting and status updates. It was only moments before their eyes got droopy, their heads started to nod, and soon there were snores rocking every room in the palace. The princesses had no sooner drifted off than sparkles took over their dreams. Blue sparkles and silver sparkles and fluorescent pink sparkles. The sparkles swirled and danced until all at once they gathered together in the shape of a beautiful, tiny fairy. Though tiny and sparkly this fairy had a voice that boomed! It was so loud that with a jolt, the snoring stopped and each princess awoke. As instructed by the fairy, they gathered together in the palatial guest room. Immediately the darkness that had been clouding the princesses' lives for days dispersed and the entire guest room was filled with sparkly light. The princesses hopped onto the guest bed (no easy task because it was prepared for another distant princess with a pea at the bottom and several mattresses on top), and started shouting questions to the dainty fairy. "Who are you?" "Are you going to give us 3 wishes?" "Are you going to outfit us for a ball?" "Do you really use fairy-

dust?" Now remember, our tiny, sparkly fairy had a booming voice. So when she opened her mouth, the rest of the room fell silent. "You don't need any fairy dust, girls. And I'm not here to grant wishes. Have you forgotten who you really are? Princess Emily and Princess Rebecca ... has it been so long since you've used your title that you forgot your royal heritage? Have you been so busy comparing your lives to each other's that your focus got diverted? I've been sent here to remind you. You, each of you, are daughters of a King! I'm not here to turn a pumpkin into a carriage and mice into footmen. I'm not here to wave a wand and outfit you for a ball. I'm here to remind you. Your Father wants you to remember. He wants you to remember every single day, every single moment. He knows it's easy to forget - and He's allowed life to be unfair because He loves you. He wants you to become. He wants you to become like His Queen. That could never happen if life were too easy. So He sent me with a message to help you remember. I'm a very busy sparkly fairy you know, so I can't come every night. This is why you must remember these instructions. Princesses, forget yourselves. When something is unfair, let it go and find someone who needs a smile. The first piece of magic I'm sharing with you is to serve. Every single day there is someone who could use a smile - and many who need more. If you focus on others, you will remember your title: Princess. The second piece of magic goes with the first. Smile! It really takes no effort at all. This is a simple trick that is often forgotten, but when practiced until it's a habit, it becomes insurance against memory loss. If you smile with your face, your heart and mind will follow and you will remember who you really are. The last piece of magic the King wants me to share with you tonight is this: You may not see Him, but He is always near. And you don't have to request a royal audience to visit with Him. It's a little piece of magic called prayer. Some of His princesses forget that prayer is appropriate and can take place anytime, anywhere. Some think that morning and evening prayers are all He's available for. My message to you is that He will grant you audience and hear your prayers any time. You can pray out loud, on your knees, in your car, in the classroom, walking, testing, thinking. Any time, any place. This last piece of magic is the most important. So important that when you wake up, I have a gift to help you remember this. The pumpkin you take with you out of this magnificent guest room will remind you that you don't need a gown or a carriage. You don't need fairy dust or footmen. You need your King. You need to remember you are His daughter. And you need to help His other Sons and Daughters remember who they are too."

The fairy finished speaking and the room was hushed. Our little princesses were in tears. They were filled with remembrance of their Royal Heritage and all of a sudden the homework, the texts, the status updates, the ripped jeans, the laundry, the babysitting, the gossipy friends ... none of it mattered. Well, they knew they'd be back in the thick of things come morning, but as they looked around at each other, the tears started to sparkle. The princesses began to glow. Their hearts swelled up and all they wanted to do was run throughout the kingdom and share the good news the sparkly, tiny fairy had shared with them! "We are all children of a King!" These young princesses all circled around, reached their hands into the center and stuck out their pinkies. "Let's pinky promise to remember - to always remember!"

And their lives went on. They all had hardships, but because they never again forgot, they all were joyful. And they lived happily ever after.

We must remember who we really are, and in so doing, remember who we are working to become. Just like fictional Alice, we will wake up one day, and realize that we are changed. We have *become*. And it may all seem like a dream, a glorious journey!

CHAPTER 6
CHOOSING WHAT DEFINES ME

We all have hardship. Everyone here could be defined by their hardship (the one with diabetes; the one who got kicked out of her apartment, etc.). Sometimes we erroneously think that we should be defined by our hardship. And often we think we don't have any control over that – after all, it *is* true. I really am lonely, or I really did embarrass myself, or I really don't have a job. Whatever it is … it may be true. But it's not who we are. We choose who we are. What others may think of us, what hardship comes our way, what struggles we're in the midst of … none of that matters when it comes to defining ourselves.

In the pre-mortal life we fought hard for the gift of choice. Now that we have it, are we using it to its fullest? Or have we given up the fight, and we're letting life just happen to us? Sure – we choose what to wear each day and where we'll go. We choose what we do in any given day. But let's start taking *choice* a few steps further. When we take control of choices we realize that we get to choose *how we feel*. We get to choose reactions to situations. We get to choose *who we are*. No one else can do that for us. We are who we decide we are. We feel how we decide to feel.

Eve and Esther both chose to define themselves. They looked toward who they wanted to become, and chose to fulfill those roles. Eve, foreordained to be the Mother of All Living, made choices that put her on that divine path. She didn't label herself as "the one who gave into the serpent," or "the one who caused misery." Instead, she boldly chose mortality and motherhood.

Had Esther let circumstances define her, she could have easily fallen into self-pity as a Jewish orphan whose dreams and ambitions would be halted because of circumstance. But instead, she rose in confidence to be the voice of her people. Both Eve and Esther teach us that we, each of us, have the right and the responsibility to choose what defines us.

My husband and I have always had high expectations of our children. And rightly so ... they're all intelligent, motivated individuals who have no reason not to succeed. When we moved to Nevada we were excited to see that the Clark County School District had a way for parents to keep up-to-date with the students' assignments, tests, and everything else: ParentLink. Each day I'd log in and take a peek at each of the children's current grades. A click of the button and I'd be taken to a particular subject to see what assignments were turned in, what the grade on the latest quiz was, and even extra-credit grades. If something hadn't been turned in I'd know right away and that day the assignment got completed before any fun activities. The kids knew we were checking grades and homework assignments daily, so for the most part they stayed on top of things. That is, until Bryan decided to "match wits" with me. At first it was just being slow getting things done. It was a struggle between us – who was the most stubborn, who would give in first. I'd take away computer privileges, limit time on the phone, and even reinforce a bed time. When he'd finally complete a missing assignment I'd play "liaison" and with my silver tongue convince the teacher to accept the tardy work. Day by day our relationship was being strained. And each day, after our "school encounter" I'd be exhausted and stressed. I'd reinforce that I love him, and he'd respond with a grunt. Finally, during the middle of Bryan's sophomore year I had an epiphany. Brad and I had spent weeks and weeks pondering, praying, studying – trying to figure out the solution. This one morning after seeing everyone off for the day, clear as a bell I realized that our relationship was way more important than any grades. If I backed off, if I eliminated myself from Bryan's school life, what's the worst that could happen? Brad and I talked and we decided the very worst thing was that he wouldn't graduate. Could we live with that? Well, when we considered that the alternative was a horrible relationship on the fast road to no relationship, then the answer was a resounding YES. We love Bryan for Bryan – not for his grades. But our job as parents is to teach him and to help him be his very best self. To help him on his road to adulthood and to an eternity of progression. What? Wait a second! Adults are responsible for their own choices. They think, then act, then have consequences. Did we really mean that we wanted Bryan to be a responsible adult? That we wanted what was best for Bryan and not for us? We were filled with immense peace and huge relief when we contemplated backing completely out of Bryan's school life. We could live with whatever he chose to do. And we would love him all the way through it. That day when Bryan came home from school, ready for the usual battle, I grabbed him and gave him a quick squeeze. "Bryan, Dad and I have a plan. Our relationship is WAY more important to us than any grades. I don't want to be the school police anymore. You're smart – if you want to succeed in school, you certainly don't need my help! We're going to give you a choice: either we can keep going like we've been going – me in your face all the time about school work; or I'll back completely out. But here's the thing: if I back out, I back all the way out. I won't check anything on ParentLink. If I get a phone call from the school I'll not answer it. If something comes in the mail, I'll put it on your bed and let you deal with it. The downside is that I won't intervene on your behalf anymore. Any teacher schmoozing will have to come from you. One more thing: if you don't graduate, or can't get in to a college, you still will have to leave home. You'll be an adult and you can't bum around and live off of us. Do you want some time to think about this?" Bryan lit up and it's as if instantly the entire world relaxed. He didn't need any time to think. The new plan was in place and life got instantly better. When he'd come home and I'd ask him how his day was, he was no longer defensive. When his dad would ask me if I knew how his grades were, it was almost comical the relief I felt as I said, "I don't know"! I didn't know – and I stopped caring. For the last two and a half years of his schooling I had no idea what his grades were. I only knew what classes he was taking because every now and then he'd tell me something interesting or funny that happened in class. As graduation drew near, I honestly didn't know if he was going to graduate. We didn't talk about it. When he told me he was leaving for graduation rehearsal I realized that I hadn't even really been thinking about it. He came home from rehearsal with his cap and gown and his tassel. His gold tassel. "I'm getting an advanced honors diploma, Mom. I'll be sitting on the first couple of rows."

We gave Bryan the opportunity to define himself. And he did. That is what our agency is about!

I learned to define myself rather than let my life define me when I was diagnosed with Multiple Sclerosis. My diagnosis was really scary, but it wasn't *me*. My experience with MS was relatively brief. I learned through my years with MS that it is my choice to let a *thing* define me, or to make the choice to define myself. I love the phrase, "I have MS, MS doesn't have me." That phrase can be tweaked for any situation: "I have financial hardship, financial hardship doesn't have me." Or "I have dating problems, dating problems don't have me." Take a minute and insert whatever has been threatening to define you – and make the switch. "I have ___, ___ doesn't have me." It's powerful, really.

William Ernest Henley, the author of the famed poem *Invictus* grew up in a home without much in the way of worldly possessions. In fact, it is said that his was "an impoverished childhood." At the age of 12, young William was stricken with Tuberculosis. It was a disease that would afflict him his entire life. However, he moved forward with life, attended school and had friends. William was a gifted writer and a good friend of Robert Louis Stevenson. As an adult, one who had lived with infirmity as well as disability, he was described by Lloyd Osbourne (Stevenson's stepson) as "... a great, glowing, massive-shouldered fellow with a big red beard and a crutch; jovial, astoundingly clever, and with a laugh that rolled like music; he had an unimaginable fire and vitality; he swept one off one's feet." You may know the story of the writing of his poem, *Invictus*. His right foot was getting more and more infected because of complications from Tuberculosis. Eventually he was hospitalized and his right leg was amputated. During the hospitalization (which lasted a full 3 years) disease and infection spread to his left leg and doctors prepared for the second amputation. But Henley called in a specialist who performed multiple surgeries and eventually was able to save Henley's leg. It was during this time that William Henley penned the words of the poem *Invictus*.

> *Out of the night that covers me*
> *Black as the pit from pole to pole*
> *I thank whatever gods may be*
> *For my unconquerable soul.*
>
> *In the fell clutch of circumstance*
> *I have not winced nor cried aloud.*
> *Under the bludgeonings of chance*
> *My head is bloody, but unbowed.*
>
> *Beyond this place of wrath and tears*
> *Looms but the Horror of the shade,*
> *And yet the menace of the years*
> *Finds and shall find me unafraid*
>
> *It matters not how straight the gate,*
> *How charged with punishments the scroll,*
> *I am the master of my fate,*
> *I am the captain of my soul.*

An interesting point of fact: Robert Louis Stevenson, shortly after the publication of Treasure Island, wrote in a letter to his friend William: "I will now make a confession: It was the sight of your maimed strength and masterfulness that begot Long John Silver ... the idea of the maimed man, ruling and dreaded by the sound, was entirely taken from you." William Ernest Henley is inspiring! I cannot imagine growing up in poverty and ill health, having a leg amputated, spending 3 years in a hospital with the threat of losing my other leg, and coming out feeling like I am the "captain of my soul." And yet … don't we each have our "dark nights" and "black pits"? Aren't we each given the opportunity (for some of us, many times over) to choose to be the masters of our fates and the captains of our own souls? I testify that this is so. Mortality is an opportunity to grow in a way we couldn't as spirits. And we all know that growth only comes through opposition. So, why would we ever choose to let the opposition define us, when really, it's what results from the opposition that makes us who we are. Isn't it so much better to look to what the opposition is creating and define ourselves that way, rather than choosing to have opposition itself be who we are? I think so!

So, how do we do it? How do we pull ourselves out of the lie that we don't have control?

- **Take Responsibility.** This means that whether I am happy or sad, excited or angry, agitated or calm … those feelings are mine and mine alone. Nothing can make me feel that way – no other person can make me feel that way. It is my choice. Eleanor Roosevelt said, "No one can make you feel inferior without your consent." That is true. And you can substitute any word in place of "inferior." No one can make you feel angry without your consent … or bitter or sad or jealous. So the next time your boss speaks in a demeaning way and your blood starts to boil; or the next time your roommate leaves dishes in the sink; or the next time a driver cuts you off … own your thoughts. Go ahead and be angry or frustrated if you want. But be honest enough with yourself to *not* blame those feelings on another person. If you're going to be angry, tell yourself that you are choosing to be angry. It's actually empowering. Once we recognize that we have control – that outside forces or people are not controlling how we feel – it's so much easier to progress and to become more charitable, more even-keeled, more patient.

- **Release Responsibility.** So, while we're at it – while we're taking responsibility for our own thoughts and feelings, let go of the erroneous belief that you can make another person happy or sad or angry or at peace. It is the other person's responsibility to choose how they feel – the same as you! If you're a people-pleaser, realize that it's good to be kind, but your kindness will not make a person happy. They will choose happiness. Or not.

- **Mind Your Own Mind.** And stay out of other people's minds. That mind-reading thing … it's unhealthy! To define yourself by what other people think is ridiculous. First: It doesn't really matter. In the end, aren't we really trying to be who Heavenly Father wants us to be? And isn't He the only one who truly knows our hearts and who we really are? Don't we want to stay true to our principles and let that define us? If that's the case, then does what other people think really have any bearing at all on who we are or what we think of ourselves? It shouldn't. Secondly: It is absolutely none of our business what others think. Their thoughts are their own – stay out of them. Chances are if you're trying to define your life by what others think, you'll be wrong anyway! Have you ever had someone tell you "You did this because you think I'm wrong"? Or anything else: being told what you think and you want to shout: THAT'S NOT WHAT I THINK! Well, we really can't know what another person thinks. And it's truly none of our business anyway. So mind your own mind, and stay out of other people's minds.

- **Recognize the Positive Changes You're Making.** Some people do this by keeping a list of things they accomplish each day. Did you study your scriptures for 3 days in a row? Get the car in for an oil change? Follow every prompting you had today? Keep a list – or write these in a journal. Then once a week, or even every day, look back on those lists of positive accomplishments and recognize that you are redefining yourself daily – in a very positive way!

- **Choose Who You Will Be.** Set goals, dream, be inspired, get direction. Don't live in the past, defining yourself by who you used to be, how you used to think, what you used to do. Define yourself by who you plan to be, who you will become. Make a dream board or To Be List. Take time in your prayers and your moments alone to imagine your future. Live in joyful anticipation with an air of excitement as you work toward who you are becoming. And as you do this, welcome the twists and turns that come your way. Then redirect your thinking as you redefine yourself bit-by-bit.

Our journeys are exciting! Each of us is on a grand adventure, specially and individually designed for us. Take charge of who you are by knowing who you want to be. And along the way, find joy. Because it's there. It's in every hardship and every success.

CHAPTER 7
FINDING OURSELVES

"Behold, I will send you Elijah the prophet before the coming of the great and dreadful day of the Lord: And he shall turn the heart of the fathers to the children, and the heart of the children to their fathers, lest I come and smite the earth with a curse." (Malachi 4:5-6)

Since the beginning of time on this Earth, there have been some who have been blessed with the gift of turning their hearts to their fathers and to their children. We know that Adam and Eve taught their children: "And Adam and Eve blessed the name of God, and they made all things known unto their sons and their daughters." (Moses 5:12) Because they "made *all things* known," they must have taught their children the absolute importance of families' being linked together eternally.

Esther, also, had her heart turned to her fathers and to her children. Were it not so, she would not have sacrificed so greatly – even risking her very life – to ensure the continuation of her people on the Earth.

Knowing who we are in a mortal sense – who we come from– is fulfillment of Malachi's prophecy. Grabbing on to the Spirit of Elijah is actually embarking on a journey. And, for some of us, it's like "taking a plunge."

We had lived on Guam for nearly a year and my husband and I hadn't been out on a date yet. I didn't know anyone I trusted enough to leave our two children with. But it was time. His company was hosting a big party out on a boat in the middle of the ocean. It was a SCUBA dive party. I had never been diving before. Ever. And it was nighttime. But I wanted to do this, and my husband wanted me to as well. He was a diving instructor, so I knew I could trust him. We went out on the boat, and when we arrived at the diving location, one by one divers jumped into the water, then disappeared as they began their dives. Well, I did as Brad instructed. Placing my left hand across my weight belt and my right hand over my regulator, I summoned up the courage and did the "giant stride" off the boat, dropping 6 feet down. I sunk down into the water, then as promised, rose back up to the top. This was a scary situation, but taking that first plunge led to scores of really amazing experiences diving in the tropics. But I had to take the plunge and get started.

I was able to do this, even though it was venturing into the unknown and was completely scary, because I trusted, I believed, I had desire, and I truly had faith in my husband.

I love the experiences recorded in The Book of Mormon - the book of Ether - about the Jaredites preparing for and then embarking on their journeys in the barges. They prepared first – the Brother of Jared knowing how the barges should be built, finding light, finding a way to get fresh air. The people followed their prophet by doing as he instructed so they could be prepared. Then they actually embarked. Much like my dive, they *just did it*. Although it was hard and really rough at times, they continued on their journey and they even found joy amidst the difficulties. In fact, they never ceased singing and praising God. "And they did sing praises unto the Lord; yea, the brother of Jared did sing praises unto the Lord, and he did thank and praise the Lord all the day long; and when the night came, they did not cease to praise the Lord." (Ether 6:9) The Jaredites were rewarded after months of bouncing around, and being buried deep into the sea, by reaching the Promised Land. Lives were saved and generations benefitted because they chose to take the plunge – they embarked! Our lives are like the Jaredites. We have a prophet to direct us, and as we follow his counsel, we are prepared to embark in the service of God. Part of that service is searching out our family histories.

Lehi's family had a similar experience to that of the Jaredites. They, also, were led to the Promised Land. But in order to get there, they had to embark. After traveling through much wilderness, they stepped onto the boat that Nephi built, and they embarked on their journey. When they were united, they made great forward progress; when they were divided, it was disastrous. They did eventually make it to the Promised Land, and it all began when they chose to embark.

In more recent history, generations were changed when the courageous Pilgrims embarked on the Mayflower. It was a dangerous journey with many losing their lives. Of those who landed, few survived that first winter in their new home. But it was the Pilgrims' embarking that was the beginning of many positive changes.

Family history and temple work is essential for the salvation of the human race. And so, we who live on the Earth today are having our hearts turned. We are taking the plunge – we are embarking as the Lord hastens His work. We are encouraged to search out our ancestors – not just their names and significant dates, but also *them*. Who were they? How did they live? What were their joys and their sorrows? Those who search and share benefit others who are just starting to look on the surface. I've been blessed to learn about my ancestors from the searching others have done.

I have one ancestor, Rube Morgan. He lived in Idaho in the old cowboy days. Those were the days when outlaws rode through on their horses and robbed banks, stole cattle … that sort of thing. Well, the town got word that a well-known outlaw was headed their way, so they gathered the men of the town and placed them in strategic locations to catch the outlaw. As it turned out, the outlaw came riding through, hopped off his horse and stole a fresh horse, then took off. While my Great Uncle Rube was waiting for the rest of his posse to arrive, here came the outlaw, galloping in his direction. There was no time to wait for the rest of the posse, so Uncle Rube hollered out for the outlaw to stop. (In my mind, I see a great western movie playing out in black and white. My Uncle Rube, the hero, rises in his stirrups and shouts: "Stop! In the name of the LAW!") But paying Uncle Rube little heed, the outlaw continued to ride. Then, without slowing down, he turned toward Uncle Rube, pulled out his gun, and shot! This outlaw either had really good aim or really bad aim, because he shot Uncle Rube's trigger finger right off his hand, then continued his escape. There are pictures of Uncle Rube in our family history with his trigger finger preserved in a jar of formaldehyde. Uncle Rube was pretty proud of his bravery!

Not all ancestral stories are as colorful as Uncle Rube's. Another ancestor, Ann Scott, was a good woman who was grateful for opportunities to do her part during the early days of the Church. She was not a major player in early Church History, but her actions during the height of persecution may be the reason we have some important church documents today. Ann recorded in her own journal: "Joseph's confinement in prison, coupled with the ruthless invasions of the mob, cause his scribe, Elder James Mulholland, to seek a place of safety for important church papers in his possession. Among the papers in Mulholland's keeping was the manuscript of the Inspired Translation of the Bible, the revelation on the rebellion, etc., etc. Bro. Mulholland requested me to take charge of these papers, as he thought they would be more secure with me, because I was a woman and the mob would not be likely to search my person. Immediately on taking possession of the papers, I made two cotton bags of sufficient size to contain them, sewing a band around the top ends of sufficient length to button around my waist; and I carried those papers on my person in the day-time, when the mob was around, and slept with them under my pillow at night. I cannot remember now the exact length of time I had those papers in my possession; but I gave them to Sister Emma Smith, the prophets [sic] wife, on the evening of her departure for Commerce [February 6 1839]." Besides this opportunity to protect precious Church papers, Ann Scott had to have endured terrible trials with the Saints. I'm grateful for this little piece of a look into her life. It tells me that she was a woman of character, fortitude and faith.

As important as seeking out our ancestors and learning about them as people, is doing their temple work for them. I've had some precious moments in the temple when I have been blessed to receive saving ordinances as I acted as proxy for my ancestors. I've felt a closeness and a true kinship. Just as in serving others with whom we come in contact every day, when we serve our ancestors and others in the temple, we are drawn out of ourselves and are filled with true joy.

In April 2014, Elder Quentin L. Cook spoke of *Roots and Branches:* "The doctrine of the family in relation to family history and temple work is clear. The Lord in initial revelatory instructions referred to baptism for your dead. Our doctrinal obligation is to our own ancestors. This is because the celestial organization of heaven is based on families. The First Presidency has encouraged members, especially youth and young single adults, to emphasize family history work and ordinances for their own family names or the names of ancestors of their ward and stake members. We need to be connected to both our roots and branches. The thought of being associated in the eternal realm is indeed glorious."

One of my brothers recently had a break-through while searching for a particular ancestor. He spoke of the journey, "As an adult, I would occasionally take a look at this mystery and poke it with a stick; but I was always confronted with the same brick wall my mother and grandmother were." He then relayed how difficult it was to locate this ancestor because of the ancestor's name. With immigration and frequent changes of the spelling of this ancestor's name, searching specifics became quite a puzzle. Through consistent effort combined with miraculous events, not only was he able to find this ancestor, but he also uncovered a whole new line that no one knew about. My brother is quick to give credit where credit is due. Not only was he directed in his search, but as he said, "The entry is something I never, ever thought I would see ... And it's all because some good volunteers sat on their couches on Sundays and 'did indexing.' Without having been indexed, there is absolutely no way this record would have come to light."

We are all at different seasons in our lives. We each have our own talents and spiritual gifts. As we prayerfully consider our role in helping secure sacred ordinances for our ancestors at *this season of our lives,* we will be inspired and we will be directed! Plunging into family history and embarking on searching out our ancestors is one way our moments in life can be put to good use!

CHAPTER 8
MORTALITY

"And as Jesus passed by, he saw a man which was blind from his birth. And his disciples asked him, saying: Master, who did sin, this man, or his parents, that he was born blind? Jesus answered, Neither hath this man sinned, nor his parents; but that the works of God should be made manifest in him." (John 9:1-4)

Do we sometimes ask ourselves: Why me? Why now? What did I do to make this happen?

Sometimes those questions are appropriate. Sometimes we need to make course corrections, to re-evaluate our methods, our motives and our actions. But often things happen in our lives that are not a direct result of our sinning or our inattention.

Both Eve and Esther could have allowed themselves to get caught up in the "Why Me's" of life! And yet – scripture tells us that these strong women focused on the task to be done. They moved forward with confidence and faith. They acted, rather than being acted upon.

Recently I was taught an important truth by one of my daughters: So much of what happens in our lives can be attributed to the simple fact that we are mortal. Of course, I've known that in my head, but finally, my whole soul learned and accepted that truth. We are mortal beings, and for no reason other than the fact that this is mortality – things happen to us. BUT, let's remember that "...all these things shall give thee experience, and shall be for thy good." (D&C 122:7) Heavenly Father can and WILL turn all things ... ALL THINGS ... to our good!

I have a friend who is a believer in the "universe." She is a good, good person who has experienced a whole lot of bad in her life. She doesn't pray to Heavenly Father, doesn't have faith in the Lord, Jesus Christ. But she does know the eternal truth that all that happens in her life can be used to lift her to greater heights. Her mantra is "Eventually I will see that this is for my greater good."

There are two truths I hope to effectively address in this chapter:

1. Absolutely everything that happens in our lives can turn for our good and project us toward becoming like Heavenly Father

2. Everything we experience can be used by the Master, "that the works of God should be made manifest in [us]."

My family and I spent 12 years in Sitka, Alaska … geographically, a paradise! The winters were cozy and dark and the summers were long and light. I loved living there … we'd sleep with our bedroom window open every night so we could hear the creek rumble in the back yard. I especially loved it when it rained at night. One summer morning I woke up after a great night sleeping to the roaring rain. I got out of bed and the outside of my leg was numb. I stood at our picture window, stomping my foot to get rid of the pins and needles. It didn't work. My leg stayed numb. As days went by the numbness spread. Eventually, it got so bad that it started to crawl up my body. It was Pioneer Day and our tiny ward was celebrating at the Church. Surprisingly, the weather cooperated. So we enjoyed an outdoor picnic with old-fashioned games. When it came time for the sack races, I joined in the fun. I climbed into the sack, the whistle blew, and I willed myself to hop. My legs refused. They just wouldn't go. I climbed out of the sack and I realized at that moment something was really wrong. I found my children and told them one at a time that I was going to head to the hospital to just get it checked out, then I asked my son, who was leaving for his mission shortly, to get the missionaries and meet me in the Relief Society room to give me a blessing. My husband was out of town – back east delivering a boat. My son was the voice for the blessing and it was exactly what I needed. Among other things, I was told that this problem was temporary, and that my experience would not only be for my good, but that it would bring about much good for other people as well. It was that phrase – that my situation would help others – that carried me through the next few years. Long story short, I was flown to Seattle to Virginia Mason Medical Center to see a neurologist who clearly diagnosed me with Multiple Sclerosis. I had so many lesions on my brain and spine that it was an easy diagnosis for him. My husband met me in Seattle so we got the diagnosis together. Although the doctor told me that MS is a lifelong, potentially debilitating disease – and that there is no cure – I knew otherwise. I didn't know how long I would have MS; I didn't know how debilitated I would get ... but I DID know that for me, it was temporary. I knew that much good could come from this, for me and for others. My 3 years with MS were difficult for me, but even more so for my family. I gave myself weekly injections, until my psyche wouldn't allow it anymore, and then our 9-year-old daughter took over and gave me the shots. The weekly injections had side effects that would put me out of commission for a full 24 hours and sometimes last up to 2 days. I learned a lot during that time. I learned to prioritize, to let go, to exercise and eat well, to take care of myself. And I learned that my experiences are NOT all about me. I learned that whatever I am going through in my life can help me reach my divine potential, which (and I believe this is true for all of us) is more about helping others than helping ourselves. And this is neat – it is not IN SPITE of MS that I have been able to be on what Elder Scott calls my "divine current" but it is BECAUSE of MS.

I had a really heart-warming, tender experience not long ago. I just received a new visiting teaching assignment. I was assigned to visit a 21-year-old girl I had never met. She moved into our ward a year or so earlier, but had been unable to attend church much because of her condition. She had terminal cancer and was in treatment more than she was out of treatment. We had her over to our home to visit with her, get to know her, and give her a change of scenery. She was a beautiful young woman who had to shift goals, desires, perspective … really, everything. Well, my daughters and I enjoyed a few minutes with her as we read a few verses out of the Book of Mormon and then talked about them. It was Alma 34 – the part where Amulek is teaching us about prayer. You know, "pray over your flocks, your households, in your closets …" After he instructs us where to pray, how to pray and what to pray about, he says this: "And now behold, my beloved brethren, I say unto you, do not suppose that this is all; for after ye have done all these things, if ye turn away the needy, and the naked, and visit not the sick and afflicted, and impart of your substance, if ye have, to those who stand in need – I say unto you, if ye do not any of these things, behold, your prayer is vain, and availeth you nothing, and ye are as hypocrites who do deny the faith. Therefore, if ye do not remember to be charitable, ye are as dross …" (Alma 34:28-29) This sweet young woman taught me an important truth. She said that our entire purpose in life is to lift others. We cannot grow by focusing only on ourselves. If we hope to become better, to progress, to be worthy to be with Heavenly Father, we have to be focused on helping others.

This girl was homebound. And yet she was still helping other people. Do you think she had any idea how, because of her cancer – and not in spite of it – she helped me? Then, at a time when she could have been asking herself, "Why me? Why now? Why couldn't I first experience a little more life?" instead she was preparing herself to go through the temple and in that preparation was teaching me – up until a few days earlier, a stranger to her – how to really live. Truly, the works of God were being made manifest in Tiffany. Whether she would be physically healed or not, His works were manifest in the miracle of Tiffany being able to share herself.

During my MS experience I was able to live mostly joyfully. It was during this time that the scripture I quoted at the beginning of this chapter about the blind man became one of my favorites. I knew that "the works of God [could] be made manifest in [me]." COULD. If I would allow it to happen. I knew, because of Priesthood blessings and because of personal revelation, that my MS was not a life-long situation for me. And so I knew that in my healing the works of God would be made manifest. I knew that the miracle that would take place in me, physically, would bring about increased faith for my family and for others. But I also knew that if I weren't going to receive that physical healing, the works of God could still be made manifest in me. I knew that even with my physical healing, the works of God were being made manifest in a lot of other ways. But it was up to me, and still is, to let others into my life and to let them have positive experiences *because* of my experience.

We each have our own set of trials and hardships. That is unique to each of us. Even if there is someone else with your same disease, in your same financial condition, whatever ... your situation is unique to you. BUT, because of Heavenly Father's omniscience and because of His love for us, what happens to us can be custom fit to our greater good. And although each of us is on our own unique journey, each of us who hopes to become celestialized will experience similar emotions and similar growth. And each of our situations will not only lead us to exaltation if we allow it, but our situations can be the means of leading others toward their exaltations.

I have a friend a little bit younger than me who has her own set of trials. In addition to her trials, she is also very busy. A mother of 21 children, 12 of them are adopted. Most of the adopted children have a disability of some sort. Now, this is what is amazing: Deanne and Doug have taught their children that whatever it is that makes them unique (ethnicity, physical deformity, traumatized early life, etc.) is a blessing to help them reach and connect with and help certain people in life. They've taught them that without their particular traits they may not be able to be an instrument to help specific people. How is that for the works of God being made manifest?!

Let's talk for a moment about the effect of our attitude on our actual trials. If we have a great attitude are our trials shortened? I don't know. But I do absolutely know that they *feel* shorter. Here is how I know this:

I grew up in a large family (by the world's standards) – probably an average size family by the Church's standards. I was #3 of 6 children, sandwiched between two brothers. We were very close in age and I often wonder how my mother did it! (Perhaps we were the reason she, even now, looks much younger than her age – we kept her hopping!) I grew up knowing I wanted a large family and I wanted my children close together so they could have what I had growing up. Well, we all know that the best planned-for lives rarely turn out that way. I remember when I was 20 actually praying that Heavenly Father would give me just a quick, 1-second view of my life as a whole so I could not worry, and know how everything would turn out. I promised that I would work really hard to grow my faith if I could just know the outcome now. ☺ Anyway, I was in my late 20s, married with one child. He was approaching age 4. This was a time in my life when I not only thought I knew what was best, but I also thought I was in control and could make things go my way. I suppose I'd had some success early in my life talking people into things … I don't know. But I do know that at that time I thought I could force things to happen my way. I can remember thinking (and this is embarrassing) "Heavenly Father, I'm sure your way is good. I'm sure that as you look at my life, you know what things will help me be strong. But let me tell you why what I want is actually the better way." And then I would go on in my mind or in my prayers to "convince" Him.

What it boils down to, really, is pride. I was proud! I was NOT humble. Why did I think (and why so often do I now think) that MY plan needs to be the way things are done? If I am not giving my will to Him, I am too proud. Neal A. Maxwell said, "As you submit your wills to God, you are giving Him the only thing you can actually give Him that is really yours to give. Don't wait too long to find the altar or to begin to place the gift of your wills upon it! No need to wait for a receipt. The Lord has His own special ways of acknowledging." *(Remember How Merciful the Lord Hath Been, April 2004 General Conference)*

We struggled with infertility our whole married lives. (We now have 5 children and several grandchildren – and each has their own miraculous story.) Well, I was an angry, infertile young woman. My attitude stunk. I was constantly looking at pregnant women, at mothers of whole broods of children and in my mind criticizing them – *She doesn't deserve those kids ... look at how she's just ignoring them; Why does she get to be pregnant with twins and I don't even get one?* – and on and on. I was like George Banks in the movie Mary Poppins, who wouldn't even recognize his grouchiness. Remember when the whole household is walking around the house humming and singing "Supercalifragilisticexpialidocious"? He said to his wife, "Winifred, will you be good enough to explain this unseemly hullabaloo?" And she says, "It's clear that you're out of sorts. We're just trying to make you feel better." And then Mr. Banks responds: "I do NOT require being made to feel better!" Well, that's how I was for a while. Eventually, after more infertility and miscarriage, Brad and I decided to adopt. When, finally, little Bryan was placed in our home as a foster child, I was appeased. I thought my trial was over. I was like a little 2-year-old who throws a temper tantrum, goes to bed angry, then when I get a candy the next day, I'm all smiles. Give me my way and I'm happy; don't and I'll punish you with frowns and crying and screaming. So, I'd had my several-year-long temper tantrum, but now that I had my way – I was happy. Until Bryan's birth parents' parental rights were terminated 8 months later and we were told that other families were being considered to be Bryan's adoptive family. Then the adult temper tantrums started all over again. I reminded myself of the blessing I'd received the night Bryan was placed in our home. It promised that Bryan was ours eternally, but cautioned that I should be patient with the time it would take to make this happen. This was 8 months earlier … *hadn't I been patient long enough?!?* Well, this was the hardest trial I have experienced in my life so far. And it's also the trial that I've learned and grown from the most. The entire journey lasted nearly 2 years. Bryan was sealed to us just 3 weeks shy of 2 years from the date he entered our home. There were so many ups and downs, so many scares, so much concern … but this was the time I grew out of temper tantrums. And although I'm not proud of how I acted and how I felt during those two years, I'm ever so grateful for Heavenly Father's patience with me. Those two years felt like 10. I wondered if it would never end. And, although we had fun times together as a family, so much of my moments during those two years were lost to frustration, anger, stress, and lack of faith. I often wonder, if I'd have developed more faith before that experience, how my memories of that time would be different. For me, those two years were torturous.

As I've compared those 2 years with my 3 years of the MS experience, it's like night and day. In both instances, the outcome was favorable. But the 3 years of MS felt like a couple of months to me. I knew that Heavenly Father knew what was best, and I also knew that my actions during that time could be of benefit to others. My faith was stronger, and I knew then – as I know now – that Heavenly Father's will is *always* best. It's easy for me to compare these two trials in my life because of their similarities: In both instances I had received a Priesthood Blessing early on. I knew the outcome would be favorable. (So why did I worry so much and stress so much with the adoption trial?) In both cases, I had no idea what the length of time would be. I knew that both situations could be and probably would be difficult. How I handled MS compared to how I handled adoption may not have made a difference in how long the trial lasted, but it made all the difference in how long it felt.

Why did Bryan have to come to us through adoption – through a contested adoption where it was the government that was contesting? I don't know – but I do know that in Bryan, the "works of God [were] made manifest" to me. I learned what faith really is. I learned that putting my trust in Heavenly Father is ultimately better than trusting another person or especially (and this was hard for me) so much better than trusting myself. I am so thankful that Heavenly Father allowed me to clumsily trudge through that experience so that I could grow. I was so self-absorbed those two years that I'm not sure I ever thought of another person. How painful that was for me!

Doesn't it hurt so much more when you think about it?!? Isn't distraction such a gift?!

When our first grandchild was not quite a year old, he stayed with us for 10 days while his parents took a little trip. We still had 3 children at home, so I had lots of help. Little Jace hadn't been weaned yet, so besides helping him get through those 10 days without his mommy and daddy to play with, we got the awesome responsibility of weaning him. That first day was really tough! Jace refused the bottle. He wouldn't eat. It was really scary! We finally found a solution: Sierra and Azure, then ages 13 and 10, would stand in front of me as I held Jace facing them. They would dance and sing like crazy people while I snuck a bottle into his face. As long as the girls were moving and making noise, Jace was distracted and drank the bottle. The second they stopped to take a breath, Jace would spit the bottle out and start screaming. It was an exhausting first 2 days until Jace got used to the bottle! But it was the distraction that allowed Jace to forget that it was Grandma with a bottle, not his mommy, who was nourishing him. And in the end, Jace (and all of us) made it through those 10 days. He actually conquered a milestone in his development, and it was distraction – thinking about someone else – that made the difference.

Let me share another example: I'll start with telling you that when I was first diagnosed with MS, my mobility wasn't great. Walking took concentration. Well, just a couple of months into the disease, I found out my sister-in-law had taken up running. When I asked her why she would think of doing such a torturous thing, her response both humbled and touched me. "When I found out you *couldn't* run, I knew that I needed to run to show my gratitude for what I have." Our conversation ended with my telling her that when the time came that I could run again, I'd join her on a 5k. (I was speaking the lingo, but actually had no clue what a 5k was.) The extent of my running was the laps around the gym we were required to do in high school. Well, that and the "running" I did on my mission a couple of different times when I was appalled at the weight I'd gained and started up an exercise regime. (Each time I'm pretty sure we quit after the first or 2nd day.) Ok. So ... nearly 3 years after I promised Patti I would run a 5k with her once I could run again, the thought came to me to give it a try. And what-do-you-know?! I could do it! I called Patti and asked her exactly what I was getting myself into ... what is a 5k anyway? Am I committing to 10 miles, or what? I was thrilled when I found out a 5k was only 3.1 miles ... thrilled until I ran that first lap around the track.

Well, I huffed and puffed and worked and worked – day after day, week after week. Finally, it was August and we were heading south to the lower 48. There was no 5k going on at the time we would be there, so Patti organized one just for me. She got sponsors and T-Shirts and everything. It was called Sun-Up Run-Down and was a sweet course all downhill. We ran that 5k, side-by-side the whole way. It was one of the nicest things that happened to me as a result of MS. Anyway – what I'm leading up to is this: A few years passed. Then one day, the thought occurred to me that, hey, maybe I should run a marathon. That's a cool thing to have on a bucket list. Oh. My. Word. Once I committed (and paid the ridiculous amount … who pays for that kind of torture anyway?) I figured I couldn't back out. So instead I trained. The regular training takes about 6 months, so I started mine 8 months before the race date. I gave myself every break I could think of - like the extra training time, and like signing up for the early start so I could be sure to make it to the end before they took down the FINISH sign. Bummer that they cancelled the early start. Well, the time came and I actually did run the marathon. "Run" being a relative term. Thanks to a friend who actually likes running marathons, I decided to dedicate every mile to someone. Mile 1 I thought about my husband and sang songs in my head that he's written; mile 2 about my Mom, and so on. Our daughter had just entered the MTC 3 days before the race, so I told her I would think about her every 5th mile. It was a great distraction – thinking about other people while I was running. I did, actually, really well for the first few miles. Then at some point, I looked around me and found I was alone. Boy! I hoped I was actually on the course still. It was raining and sleeting and blowing and miserable. I heat up really fast, so the horrid weather was good for me – kept me cool and kept me running to stay warm. When I hit mile 20 I was so happy! I looked at the time and realized I'd make it to the finish line before the sign came down. I thought, in fact, I could pick up my speed now. Just yards past the 20-mile marker my body protested. *NO MORE!* it seemed to shout. All of a sudden I felt every single pain. I was bent forward and, thankfully, my feet were still moving so the forward position of my body meant I was making progress. At one point I saw a lucky penny on the ground, bent over to pick it up hoping it would do me some psychological good the last few miles, and actually ended up doing a somersault. No more lucky pennies for me! I was finally at mile 25 with just a little over a mile to go and I really, truly thought I couldn't finish. Then I remembered that it was Sierra's mile. Time to think about Sierra. "Called to Serve" and other missionary songs entered my mind. I thought of her studying her language and learning about Preach My Gospel. I thought of the experiences I knew she would have when she left the MTC. I thought of her loving spirit and how the entire country would be blessed because of her. I thought of her as a little child. I prayed for her. I remembered some of my hard experiences on my mission, and in the MTC, and I found myself praying out loud for Sierra. (I really was the only one around, so I could do that.) Then, all of a sudden, I saw the FINISH sign. Sierra – particularly forgetting myself and thinking about Sierra – had gotten me through that last mile. It was thinking about someone else each mile that made that marathon doable. I know that! I could not have completed it if I had focused on myself. When I was thinking about myself, I was doing stupid things like bending over to pick up pennies and then rolling over myself. When I was focused on someone else I was making progress myself.

Our lives are like this. We *will* get through our hardships one way or another. We may tumble and stumble – or we may do it more gracefully, and while helping others through prayer or action, we will be moving forward toward our goal and toward the end of the trial.

Remember the people of Alma? They lived in the city they named Helam and they were righteous people. They were living good lives, and peaceful lives – tilling the land – when they were attacked and taken into bondage. They had done nothing to deserve this! (Mosiah 23) But still, they were taken into bondage. And it was tough. And they could see no end. And they were ordered to stop praying (Mosiah 24:11). But "... Alma and his people did not raise their voices to the Lord their God, but did pour out their hearts to him; and he did know the thoughts of their hearts." Then remember what happens? They aren't released from bondage yet. Instead, as they pray in their hearts, the Lord tells them, "... I will ease the burdens which are put upon your shoulders, that even you cannot feel them upon your backs, even while you are in bondage ..." Imagine the peace they felt! Then it happened. "And now it came to pass that the burdens which were laid upon Alma and his brethren were made light; yea, the Lord did strengthen them that they could bear up their burdens with ease ..." Now this is important: " ... and they did submit cheerfully and with patience to all the will of the Lord." (Mosiah 24:14-15) And then – *after all this* – they are led out of bondage! Do you think this experience changed the people of Alma? Do you think the Lord was able to make their burdens easier to bear *because* they let the Lord in? I do. Do you think that the Lord will make **our** burdens light if we allow Him to? And do you think that His works were made manifest in them? Let's see ... Mosiah welcomes them into the Land of Zarahemla. Mosiah chapter 25, verses 8 and 10: The people of Mosiah "knew not what to think; for when they beheld those that had been delivered out of bondage they were filled with exceedingly great joy ... and again, when they thought of the immediate goodness of God, and his power in delivering Alma and his brethren out of the hands of the Lamanites and of bondage, they did raise their voices and give thanks to God." Mosiah's people were lifted and enlightened and inspired *because* of the trial that Alma's people had endured.

I know that as we allow Heavenly Father's will to lead us on our individual divine currents, His works will be made manifest in us. And as we focus on lifting others and loving others, regardless of what is going on in our lives, we will be propelled further along our road of eternal progress.

CHAPTER 9
LIFT WITH YOUR LEGS

In speaking to the Priesthood brethren in the October 2008 General Conference, President Dieter F. Uchtdorf talked of service. His address, *Lift Where You Stand*, emphasized the truth that we are all needed. He taught that position is irrelevant. We are needed to fulfill our callings and opportunities to serve at every stage of our lives, in every position we have. "When we seek to serve others, we are motivated not by selfishness but by charity. This is the way Jesus Christ lived His life and the way a holder of the priesthood must live his. The Savior did not care for the honors of men; Satan offered Him all the kingdoms and glory of the world, and Jesus rejected the offer immediately and completely. Throughout His life, the Savior must have often felt tired and pressed upon, with scarcely a moment to Himself; yet He always made time for the sick, the sorrowful, and the overlooked. In spite of this shining example, we too easily and too often get caught up in seeking the honors of men rather than serving the Lord with all our might, mind, and strength."

Neither Eve nor Esther sought for their positions. Eve was foreordained to be Adam's wife and the mother of us all. That huge responsibility required sacrifice of her own will and pleasure, her own comfort and life of ease. In Esther's case, she did not choose to become the Queen. In fact, it was a scary undertaking. Yet she used the role she had been placed in to serve in a magnificent way.

President Uchtdorf taught us to lift where we stand. In adding to his message, this chapter suggests some of the proper ways to lift.

During a confusing stage of my life when I really didn't want to live by faith – I just wanted a quick look into my future – I just knew I could be a better person if only I could get some clear direction. But there were no 10-second visions, no nighttime dreams revealing my future. I was stuck. I had to figure it out. But not on my own ... His help would come, but it wouldn't be handed to me on a cinematic screen. It would come to me as I painfully grew my faith, as I took steps into the dark, as I turned my will over to Him, and as I worked really, really hard.

Which choices I made and the directions I went aren't really important to anyone but me and my posterity. But the process of moving forward and the things I learned along the way are applicable to all of us, at every season of our lives.

We all know what it's like to try to lift something heavy ... we reach down and grab and ... YIKES. It doesn't budge. And so we change the approach. First, we look around, hoping to find a strong Andre-the-Giant type of person who will effortlessly lift it for us, but when we find ourselves alone, we reevaluate our process. With no hand truck or other means to assist, ultimately, we engage the use of our powerful legs. We bend our knees, crouch down, wrap our arms around the object, then give all the work to our legs as our knees slowly unbend, object in our arms, and we arise.

I had one such incident before I had ever even been taught the valuable "lift with your legs, not your back" principle. I was 8-years-old. I grew up in a family with 5 siblings – the oldest was 12, the youngest just a few months old. Sandwiched between two brothers, one a year and a half older than me, the other was only fifteen months younger. But as soon as he reached toddler-hood he had a growth spurt that made it look like I was the younger one. He was always bigger than me – but I was faster. ☺ Well, one summer day we were all playing – some inside and some outside. My mother was not only crazy-busy with her children, but she was also busy serving in the Church, which sometimes would tie her to the corded telephone. The smart mother that she was, she could multi-task like no other, and really knew how to enlist our help, too. This day, while on the phone, I was zipping through the kitchen to grab a snack. She put her hand over the mouthpiece, turned to me and quickly said, "Denalee, please go pick up Michael and bring him to me … quickly, now." I stood there and just stared. We knew better than to interrupt Mom when she was on the phone, but I couldn't imagine how I would pick up Michael! He was a couple of inches taller and more than a couple of pounds heavier than I was! So I just stood there. Hand over the mouthpiece again, my mother whispered urgently, "Now sweetie! Go get him!" So off I went. I found Michael outside doing whatever it is boys do to get so dirty, walked over and reached down to pick him up. "What are you *doing?* Leave me alone!" Well, I was obedient … and apparently Michael was too, because when I explained that Mom told me to come pick him up and carry him to her, he complied. And we didn't cheat. He didn't walk almost to Mom then make it look like I was carrying him … nope … none of that! After a few tries, I found that as I used my legs, I could lift the guy. It was a struggle, but as I grunted and shuffled forward with my heavy load, eventually I reached the kitchen. My mom quickly hung up the phone when she saw us. "What in the world are you doing? You'll hurt yourself!" I explained that I was just doing as she asked. Turns out, she meant to ask me to pick up *Darryn* and carry the baby to her. Ooops.

There is a reason we lift with our legs and not our backs. Our legs are strong! When bent the right way, as our body moves in motion with our legs, they give us leverage that multiplies our strength. Although our entire body is used to lift the object, it's our bent legs that provide the muscle and carry they heaviest part of the load.

I find it interesting that first we need to bend our legs and lower ourselves in order to properly lift. Isn't life like that? When there is something that needs to be done, a heavy load that we must carry, someone to help, a burden to bear … if we first bend our knees and lower ourselves in humble prayer, we gain leverage. Somehow, the burden is dispersed and we don't lift or carry it alone on our own backs. Even when the burden is so heavy we can almost feel the physical weight of it on our shoulders, it's our kneeling in prayer, bending our will to Heavenly Father's, that is what makes it even possible to lift. And we not only lift – we move forward.

Forward momentum is required! Lifting and then just standing still, gets exhausting and almost unbearable. We start to shake and sometimes buckle under the weight. But when we lift properly – that is, with Heavenly Father's help, by beginning on bended knee, then humbly accepting His direction and His will – and we move forward toward our goal, it's not quite so heavy. We're lifting with a purpose, keeping our eyes on our destination and knowing we will be able to soon unload. It gives us strength.

There's one more important element: We have to be looking upward and forward. Taking our eyes off the goal, for whatever reason, can also be the cause of our buckling or stumbling. The weight we carry, the loads and burdens we may have lifted and are able to bear with His help – those can become too heavy, we can become unbalanced, and stumble and fall if we forget where we're headed.

I had an experience a couple of years ago. I had done proper preparation, had "lifted with my legs," so to speak, was moving forward, but became distracted. I turned from looking forward, took my attention and placed it elsewhere, and then I paid the price. I mentioned in an earlier chapter that for some insane reason I decided to train for and run a marathon. I started 8 months before the big race with a goal: I would finish the marathon before they took down the FINISH sign. I know there are career marathoners who try to beat their best time each race … but I'm not one of them. I did my research: They keep the sign up for 6 hours, have an announcer at the finish line, music blaring, crowds cheering. As marathoners run under the big banner, arms held high and a skip in their step as adrenaline gives them that extra spurt at the end, the medal is placed over their head and photos are taken. There's a big party at the end with performers and food. Well, I did everything right for 8 months. I created the success in my mind, envisioning the course and myself running it. I pictured an exhausted me getting a burst of strength to run triumphantly through the finish line. And I worked hard. I followed the training program strictly, even on days I really, really didn't want to run. I enlisted the help of family who would sometimes run with me. It was 8 months with my eye on a goal and the determination to succeed. The day came for the marathon. I was pumped up and prepared. I ran, I jogged, I walked, I ran some more. By about mile 20 my body started to rebel big-time. I stumbled along … alone as far as I knew. I talked myself through it – every mile marker I came upon I envisioned what that meant, and tried to psyche myself out: *That's only the distance from home to the park … you've done that a million times … easy! .. just walk it, you have the time*. I was moving forward. Slowly, but still, I was going forward. In fact, I was actually bent forward and was unsure how many days would pass before I could be completely upright again. But I kept going. Up ahead I saw the next mile marker. I was getting close! I could do this! And then, I saw a little glitter out of the corner of my eye. I looked down. There, on the ground just feet ahead of me was the "lucky penny" we talked about in an earlier chapter. When I got to the penny I looked straight down, bent a little to pick it up, and the forward momentum my body was used to, combined with the weight of running 20+ miles, sent me into a somersault. I tumbled right on over and completely missed the penny. Taking my attention away from the goal, looking down, trying to stop my forward momentum … it was disastrous. It made getting up and continuing a lot harder. I was able to do it – and I did, actually, finish the marathon – but it was so much harder to start again from on the ground, than if I had never looked down and tried to stop the momentum.

Aren't our lives like that? We prepare, we focus, we pray for help, we move forward, we lift, we help, we serve. But distraction is a tool of Satan. If we forget for a moment what we're really working towards, why we're carrying the burdens we are, and where we're going … and if we allow that distraction to change our direction, even for a moment, we stumble. Everything becomes harder. We have to pick ourselves up, in our broken state, and get going again. And it's tough. It's really, really hard. Funny thing about distractions: In the case of my "lucky penny" I told myself that it might help me … it could be just the break I need. Satan tries to be tricky like that. With people who are trying to live the best we can, the distractions he throws at us are subtle … and they're brilliantly planned lies. He makes them look attractive, or logical. Anything to grab our attention and take our focus away from looking up and ahead. He wants us to look down, to get side-tracked. And he's really good at it. But, just like during my marathon, every one of us can get back up. It hurts a little, after stumbling and tumbling. But we can do it. And we can finish triumphantly, having learned from our mistakes.

Something else that I think is really important about lifting with our legs and moving forward: Everything … absolutely *everything* … is hard. Even joyful, happy things, happy times, great seasons of our lives, answers to prayers, upcoming opportunities … it's all hard! There's a really good reason for that. If things weren't hard, we would turn into mush. When resistance is removed, we atrophy. So I've learned to stop praying for things to be easy. It's simply not part of mortality. And even if it were, the easy way will only make for longer, tougher progression later. So when I remember that, when I keep it in the back of my mind that life is meant to be hard, I find myself more able to keep positive. Because remember, life is also meant to be joyful. In fact, we're told numerous times in the scriptures to be of good cheer, to have joy, and to choose happiness. So can happiness and difficulty exist at the same time? It absolutely can! I believe that is what mortality actually *is*. It's happiness amidst hardship.

If I had expected the marathon to be easy and pleasant, I imagine I would have become really grumpy and just quit – pulled out of the race – only a few miles into it. But I knew. I knew it would be hard! I knew it would be taxing. And I did it anyway. And because my expectation was that it would be hard, that I would hurt, that I would have to push myself to my very limits to finish ... I was able to find enjoyment through the entire event. I saw the beauty around me. I laughed at conversations I heard. I actually enjoyed the exhilaration of achievement. I was touched by a stranger who stepped out into the rain to shout words of encouragement and to give us snacks. There was so, so, so much good during the marathon. But never once was it easy.

President Thomas S. Monson said, "The history of the Church in this, the dispensation of the fullness of times, is replete with the experiences of those who have struggled and yet who have remained steadfast and of *good cheer* as they have made the gospel of Jesus Christ the center of their lives. This attitude is what will pull us through whatever comes our way. *It will not remove our troubles from us but rather will enable us to face our challenges, to meet them head-on, and to emerge victorious.*" *(I Will Not Fail Thee Nor Forsake Thee, October 2013 General Conference)* This is what my marathon was like – my marathon which has been a reminder about life.

So, in our lives, what are our expectations? When we expect good things to just be handed to us; when we expect life to be easy; when we expect the reward without the effort – we become dissatisfied, grumpy, discouraged, entitled. We begin to feel that life isn't fair. We start to compare ourselves with others and sometimes we murmur. We lose our ability to be grateful, and we stop recognizing Heavenly Father's hand in our lives. We become miserable. And then the spiral starts. Self-pity, self-loathing, self-rejection. And a weird thing: ego takes over. We forget our divinity, but we exalt ourselves. We look at others and think that they don't deserve all the good that's going on in their lives – that should be mine! We criticize others even while despising ourselves. It's a twisted lie that Satan puts into our hearts, making us think we're better and more deserving than someone else, and at the same time being disgusted with ourselves. The reality is that we are all on equal footing. Each one of us is divine! We are all loved and cherished by the King of Kings! President Uchtdorf said, "One of the adversary's methods to prevent us from progressing is to confuse us about who we really are and what we really desire." *(Oct. 2013, "You Can Do It Now!")* We must remember who we are, and when we do that, we remember where we are going.

We are all at exciting times in our lives! Our choices are seemingly limitless. What to study, where to live, which career path to choose, who to date, who to marry, what to become. It's very exciting. And it's confusing. But we do not have to make those choices alone. I often think of how disastrous my life would have become if there had not been some Divine direction. With my limited experience, exposure, and understanding I could have been, and would be, making a complete mess of my life. But doesn't it take a lot of the pressure off and dispel unnecessary stress when we realize that Heavenly Father doesn't just know everything about everything … but He also knows everything about *you*? He knows how you think, what you've been through, your potential, and *who you really are*. Truly, He knows us better than we know ourselves. And so, why in the world would we try to "go it alone"? It makes no sense. Is there anyone here who would try to install a garbage disposal without YouTubing it first? Or at least reading the directions? Doesn't it just make sense that we go to the experts, then follow their directions?

There's something really, really cool about the way Heavenly Father directs us. Of course, we have the scriptures and our Patriarchal Blessings to give us guidelines. But what I love … what I really, really love … is that Heavenly Father can and *will* turn all things for our good. If we allow it. Now, He doesn't want us to be miserable, and He hurts when we hurt. But He not only soothes the stings, but He turns those hard things to our best good.

And so, what does all this mean for you? I testify to you that Heavenly Father knows you. He knows your talents, and desires that you use them to lift others. Lift where you stand! It is no accident that you're in this stage of life, in this location, among these people at this time. You not only have an over-all divine purpose … you have a purpose *right now, right here*. You get this mortal experience just once. You get to be young single adults, or new parents, or empty nesters, or whatever your season is - only right now. You get today and this moment only once … and you have a purpose in every moment of every day of every stage of your life. Heavenly Father knows that purpose, and if you strive to be in tune, you will know it too. Maybe not in a grand way … but you will have peace in your heart as you follow inspiration, promptings, little whispers from the Spirit. When you do that, you are fulfilling your purpose in that moment. There are people around you, equally loved by Heavenly Father, who need you. They need you to lift them. And funny thing: it's impossible to lift someone without rising yourself. Lift where you stand! Don't let a single moment pass you by.

When I consider lifting where we stand, and being sure to lift with our legs, not our backs, I think of young Mormon. He was thrust into taking a serious approach to life at a very young age. And he took on responsibility that was greater than most of us can imagine. Consider, at age 10 Mormon knew the sacred records would someday become his responsibility. The very next year he left with his family. They moved to Zarahemla where "the whole face of the land had become covered with buildings, and the people were as numerous almost, as it were the sand of the sea." (Mormon 1:7) Many of us know what it's like to be the new kids in the neighborhood. Some of us have experienced the pain of leaving behind everything familiar. But then, just as Mormon's family gets settled, a war breaks out. A little bit of time passes where, even though there is finally peace, "wickedness did prevail upon the face of the whole land ..." (Mormon 1:13) Then at 15 years of age, Mormon is charged with leading the Nephite army! Mormon loved his people. He preached to them, he led them. I don't believe there were very many seasons in Mormon's life that were not filled with trials. Yet as I read the few chapters in Mormon in the Book of Mormon, I cannot help but be struck because of the majesty of this man, and his willingness to "lift where he stands." Truly, Mormon knew to lift with his legs. He was a man who knew that strength came from the Lord.

Now, it is quite possible to be lifting others while still fulfilling your needs. Clean your house, take an online course, go to the gym ... and all the while, be aware of thoughts and feelings that pop up. Remember, "I will tell you in your mind and in your heart ... this is the spirit of revelation." (Doctrine and Covenants 8:2-3)

Remember that Heavenly Father will guide you — but it would defeat the purpose of mortality for Him to show you everything.

And so don't be afraid to move forward before you have all the answers. There are very few people who stepped into college knowing every class they would take, which degree they would get, and then graduated exactly on time and took their dream job. There are so many twists and turns along our paths. How you view those twists and turns will make all the difference. It's an adventure, really! Go forward in the way you feel inspired, then push just as hard when life throws you a curve and you need to change directions.

Education, career, church service and relationships all require heavy lifting. If you try to do it alone, and you lift with your back ... you will most assuredly get hurt. But if you "lift with your legs, not your back" by kneeling in prayer and bending your will to Heavenly Father's, you will have the strength necessary to carry the heavy burdens of this stage of your life. You will be able to get momentum as you press forward, even without having all the answers. And regardless of the weight of the load you carry, you will be able to enjoy. There is so much wonder and goodness during every stage of life. Allow yourself to feel the light and then to share it.

King Benjamin taught, "And also, ye yourselves will succor those that stand in need of your succor; ye will administer of your substance unto him that standeth in need; and ye will not suffer that the beggar putteth up his petition to you in vain, and turn him out to perish ... For behold, are we not all beggars? Do we not all depend upon the same Being, even God, for all the substance which we have, for both food and raiment, and for gold, and for silver, and for all the riches which we have of every kind? And behold, even at this time, ye have been calling on his name, and begging for a remission of your sins. And has he suffered that ye have begged in vain? Nay; he has poured out his Spirit upon you, and has caused that your hearts should be filled with joy, and has caused that your mouths should be stopped that ye could not find utterance, so exceedingly great was your joy. And now, if God, who has created you, on whom you are dependent for your lives and for all that ye have and are, doth grant unto you whatsoever ye ask that is right, in faith, believing that ye shall receive, Oh, how ye ought to impart of the substance that ye have one to another." (Mosiah 4:16-21) Each one of us has trials. Each of us needs help. And each of us can provide help to others, regardless of the situation we are in or our season of life. When we focus on lifting where we stand and lifting with our legs – that is, in our current circumstance and with God's help – we will truly be happy, and we will progress as He desires of us.

Sometimes our service will be just a smile, or a kind word. There's a story that has floated around for years.

> A young girl was late getting home from school one day. Her mother was understandably worried, so when the girl walked in the door, the mother immediately approached her. After a big hug and a silent prayer of gratitude, the mother sharply questioned her daughter: "Why," she asked, "didn't you come straight home? I was so worried about you!" The girl told her mother that she did come straight home! But her friend who was accompanying her dropped her doll and it broke all to pieces. Thinking she understood now, the mother softly said, "Oh. So you stopped to help her pick up the pieces." "No," responded the daughter, "I stopped to help her cry."

As we strive to lift where we stand, and do so by bending our legs and beginning on our knees, we will be led through inspiration to be His angels, acting in His behalf. Can YOLO have any better meaning than that?

CHAPTER 10
IT'S A BEAUTIFUL WORLD

We all have tough days, right? You know what I'm talking about … one little thing starts the marble rolling and before you know it, absolutely everything is going wrong! On those days our To Do Lists just keep growing and growing, with nothing getting crossed off. Everyone around us exudes grumpiness. I had a day like that years ago. It was a Sunday. The power was out at our house, so we overslept our alarms and had to scramble to get out of the apartment and to church on time. Our 4-year-old was obsessed with pretty hair. While filling a bottle for the baby, searching for shoes for our son, and gathering snacks to keep the kids quiet in church, our little girl was screeching in her high pitched voice that she needed her hair fixed. It was true overload! And things didn't get better once we got to church. Our daughter cried so much through church that a doctor in the ward promised to stop by later and look into her ears. "I'm sure she's got an ear infection or something," he said. *Just go along with him*, I thought. One thing after another made me so grateful when Monday came around. It was one of those impossible days … a day I hoped to never repeat!

On those days when all is gloomy, when there is no brightness or lightness or joy, we need to dig deep to release all that negativity. And there are lots of good tricks out there – things that really work!

Do you suppose that Eve or Esther had tough days? Most certainly they did! They were mortal too … I'm sure they had "bad hair days" and worse. I mean, talk about family struggles … how Eve handled the things that happened among the children in her household, I can only imagine. And yet, Eve found joy and happiness amidst the muck. "And Eve, his wife, heard all these things, and was glad, saying: Were it not for our transgression we never should have had seed, and never should have known good and evil, and the joy of our redemption, and the eternal life which God giveth unto all the obedient." (Moses 5:11) Eve, who had experienced the Garden of Eden – a beauty that far surpasses what we know – was able to see good and beauty in the fallen world.

I imagine Esther's situation may have been really scary for her. We know she was orphaned at some point, because she was later adopted by Mordecai. What sadness she had to endure at a young age, we do not know. And then, being taken to the palace and living a year in a state of purification with people who were strangers to her ... that had to be frightening! Yet the fact that she obtained favor from all who even saw her – this tells me that she looked at the world as an optimist. She chose to see beauty and to see good. She was happy and her light emanated from her. People were drawn to Esther.

My mother told me once about a lesson she learned about "lumps." There are all kinds of lumps. Lumps in our oatmeal, lumps in our throat, breast lumps. When we have proper perspective, we can pull ourselves out of self-pity and downward spiraling to lift ourselves into a state of gratitude and acceptance. We may be complaining heavily about a lump in our oatmeal, forgetting to be grateful that we have no lumps in the breast.

I am in awe of Joseph Smith's family. When I read about their lives, I am overcome with gratitude, humility, and a bit of shock and shame as I realize how miniscule my trials are compared with what they endured. Theirs were days of never-ending pain, interspersed with glorious joy. Mother Smith was amazing. Although she speaks freely of the trials and pains in their lives, never does she sound like she is complaining. And the only place I've ever read of one of the Smiths pleading because of trials is in the Doctrine and Covenants, sections 121 and 122. We all know the Lord's answer to the Prophet Joseph Smith when he asks, "O God, where art thou? And where is the pavilion that covereth thy hiding place?" (Doctrine and Covenants 121:1) First the Lord comforts him saying, "My son, peace be unto thy soul." And then He teaches the importance of trials and afflictions. Among other things the Lord says, "... know thou, my son, that all these things shall give thee experience, and shall be for thy good. The Son of Man hath descended below them all. Art thou greater than he? Therefore, hold on thy way, and the priesthood shall remain with thee; for their bounds are set, they cannot pass. Thy days are known, and thy years shall not be numbered less; therefore, fear not what man can do, for God shall be with you forever and ever." (Doctrine and Covenants 122:7-9)

In the midst of lives sprinkled with adversity and pain, we must remember, "... men are that they might have joy." (2 Nephi 12:22) Heavenly Father sent us to Earth, in part, to experience adversity. He knows that is what will make us strong. But this life isn't supposed to be all hard knocks and pain. He wants us to be happy! He wants us to feel joy. Are trials and joy at two different ends of the spectrum? And can they not be experienced at the same time? The scriptures teach us that we can be at peace and experience joy even while enduring trials.

Hannah of the Old Testament had been barren for years. It was such a trial to her that she was "provoked ... sore, for to make her fret ..." (1 Samuel 1:6). Finally, after a great show of faith, Hannah conceived and bore Samuel. Once Samuel was weaned, Hannah took him to Eli at the temple and said, "For this child I prayed; and the Lord hath given me my petition which I asked of him; Therefore also I have lent him to the Lord; as long as he liveth he shall be lent to the Lord. And he worshipped the Lord there." (1 Samuel 1:27-28) Separating from her son had to be a great trial to this righteous woman. It could not have been easy. But the next verse in the Bible reads, "And Hannah prayed, and said, My heart rejoiceth in the Lord, mine horn is exalted in the Lord: my mouth is enlarged over mine enemies; because I rejoice in thy salvation." (1 Samuel 2:1) While at the very beginning of the trial of being separated from her young son, Hannah found joy. Perhaps it is actually grabbing onto joy that helps us endure our crosses and helps us to see that it really is a beautiful world after all! Maybe joy is essential to our successfully learning and growing from our trials.

Mary, the mother of Jesus, shared similar thoughts as Hannah. After conceiving the Child, she went to live for a time with her cousin, Elisabeth. Mary was in the midst of a trial ... she was expecting a child, but not yet married to Joseph. I don't think that in our day we can even come close to comprehending the enormity of her trial. But Mary was able to feel peace. She said, " ... My soul doth magnify the Lord. And my spirit hath rejoiced in God my Saviour ..." (Luke 1:46-47)

Though our lives may seem at times blanketed with adversity, there is joy seeping through the cracks. We just have to see it. It is not as elusive as it may seem. Often while enduring seemingly unbearable trials, the Lord will send us peace and joy.

142

We can grab onto those moments of pure joy and they will help to sustain us and help us see the good and beauty in life.

If we hope to sit down with Heavenly Father's righteous children, with our Heavenly Parents and with our Elder Brother, we must endure our crosses. Adversity will come to us. It is part of mortality. And it is in enduring these things that we are not only strengthened, but also refined. Brigham Young, in speaking to the saints in Salt Lake City said, "You all know that the Saints must be made pure, to enter into the celestial kingdom. It is recorded that Jesus was made perfect through suffering. If he was made perfect through suffering, why should we imagine for one moment that we can be prepared to enter into the kingdom of rest with him and the Father without passing through similar ordeals?" (Discourses of Brigham Young 8:66) At another gathering of the saints he said, "All intelligent beings who are crowned with crowns of glory, immortality, and eternal lives must pass through every ordeal appointed for intelligent beings to pass through, to gain their glory and exaltation. Every calamity that can come upon mortal beings will be suffered to come upon the few, to prepare them to enjoy the presence of the Lord. If we obtain the glory that Abraham obtained, we must do so by the same means that he did ... Every trial and experience you have passed through is necessary for your salvation." (Discourses of Brigham Young 8:150) This doesn't mean that we will have the exact same trials that Abraham did. We will have our own. We will still, though, need to go through the same refining process that Abraham, and all the holy people who have proven themselves, have gone through. To be refined, we must have adversity. But there is joy to be found in *every* situation. And there is beauty always surrounding us.

I learned years ago how to make pita pockets. This specialty bread has the same ingredients as other bread: flour, yeast, water. But what makes it become a pocket instead of regular bread is the high heat it is exposed to. When I first read the recipe I thought, *I can't do that – it will burn and ruin the bread!* Here's what happens: for exactly one minute you place the flattened circles of dough on a cookie sheet on the lowest rack of an oven heated to 500 degrees. 500 degrees! That is HOT. And the rule is: NO PEEKING. After exactly one minute you move the dough to an upper level and bake for an additional 3 or 4 minutes. The recipe warns: *Don't skip the one minute intense heat at the beginning or the bread will not make a pocket. And don't peek.* The first time I made the pockets I did as instructed. After one minute I moved the dough up a few levels and thought, *This goofy recipe! Nothing is happening to the dough. It's as flat as when I put it in.* I turned on the oven light about 2 minutes into the second phase and to my amazement the dough puffed and turned into an awkwardly shaped ball. We had delicious pita pocket sandwiches for lunch that day.

Our lives are much like pita pockets. Sometimes the heat is so intense we wonder how we can possibly survive. Additionally, we wonder what good the heat can possibly do for us. Yet just as the pita pockets reached their potential *after* the battle with heat, it usually takes us a while – perhaps well into the next life – to see just how essential that heat was for us.

Elder Neal A. Maxwell said, "How can there be later magnification without our enduring some present deprivation? The enlarging of the soul requires not only some remodeling, but some excavation … How could there be refining fires without our enduring some heat?" (Ensign, May 1990 p.34)

Because we are told to liken all scripture unto ourselves, it is very comforting to read the words of the Lord to Joseph Smith while he was in Liberty Jail. "My son, peace be unto thy soul; thine adversity and thine afflictions shall be but a small moment; And then, if thou endure it well, God shall exalt thee on high; thou shalt triumph over all thy foes." (Doctrine and Covenants 121:7-8)   It is so reassuring to know that God is mindful of each of us in our afflictions even though they are but for "a small moment." And the thought that we will "triumph over all [our] foes" is a wonderful blessing. Whether our foes consist of having an angry heart, or pain of rejection; physical limitations or unkindness shown to us – whatever our foes are, we will triumph. Yes, we must all have adversity. But because of a loving Father who gave His Son, none of us need carry our crosses alone. He will help us and the time will come when we will be recognized as those who "have endured the crosses of the world … and [our] joy shall be full forever." (2 Nephi 9:18)

Through all of the afflictions, trials, and hardship that come our way, the world around us hasn't changed. It is *still beautiful!* Isn't everything so much nicer when we're surrounded by beauty?! Well, the beauty is there. We just need to see it.

Listed below are little tricks I've found that have helped me when life seems to lose its beauty:

- **Count Your Blessings.** This is trite, but truly works. Whether we're struck with sudden illness, get a flat tire when we're already late to the appointment, have a family of sick youngsters, or fail a test. It may feel like

145

the whole world is crashing in on us, but if we take a moment to be grateful, beauty will return and we will better be able to endure. Remember years ago when keeping a "Gratitude Journal" was trendy? That's one trend that should endure. Those who participated took time every morning or every evening and listed five things they were grateful for that day. It's a good practice! "When was the last time you thanked the Lord for a trial or tribulation? Adversity compels us to go to our knees; does gratitude for adversity do that as well?" *(Gratitude: A Path to Happiness, Bonnie D. Parkin, April 2007 General Conference)* I wonder – if I actually *thanked* Heavenly Father, in prayer, not just *during* my difficult times, but actually *for* my difficult times, will I better be able to see the beauty around me? I think so. I think perspective would change and everything would be brighter.

- **Distract Yourself.** Sometimes all we need in order to pull us out of a dark place is some distraction. Go for a jog, call a friend, serve someone. Pulling out of ourselves and focusing our attention somewhere else is a great remedy for lifting away from darkness and into light.
- **Essential Oils.** The Lord has given us an entire Earth for our benefit. If I could have a huge garden of fragrant plants, when I was feeling down I'd go hide among the flowers and just breathe deeply. But since I don't have that, I use what is available in this day and age. Other people have extracted the essential oil from many beautiful plants. The oils serve to lift me out of my negativity and into a brightness that opens up the beauty of my world.

- **Positive Affirmations.** This is another one of those "trite" things that actually works. During a time of clear thinking, jot down some positive affirmations to draw on when it's hard to see anything in a positive light. When adversity strikes, open the list and repeat the affirmations over and over again. It really works!

President Gordon B. Hinckley said, "In all of living, have much fun and laughter. Life is to be enjoyed, not just endured." *(Stand True and Faithful, April 1996 General Conference)* It's pretty hard to live YOLO if we're stuck in a mire of gloom. Find what works for you, and choose happiness! Choose, no matter what life throws at you, to see the beauty that is *already there.*

CHAPTER 11
YOLO

"We all owe a great debt of gratitude to Eve. In the Garden of Eden, she and Adam were instructed not to eat of the tree of the knowledge of good and evil. However, they were also reminded, 'Thou mayest choose for thyself.' (Moses 3:17) The choice was really between a continuation of their comfortable existence in Eden, where they would never progress, or a momentous exit into mortality with its opposites: pain, trials, and physical death in contrast to joy, growth, and the potential for eternal life. In contemplating this choice, we are told, 'And when the woman saw that the tree was good for food .. and a tree to be desired to make her wise, she took of the fruit thereof, and did eat, and also gave unto her husband with her, and he did eat.' (Moses 4:12) And thus began their earthly probation and parenthood.

"After the choice was made, Adam voiced this grateful expression: 'Blessed be the name of God, for because of my transgression my eyes are opened, and in this life I shall have joy, and again in the flesh I shall see God.' (Moses 5:10)

"Eve made an even greater statement of visionary wisdom after leaving the Garden of Eden: 'Were it not for our transgression, we never should have had seed, and never should have known good and evil, and the joy of our redemption, and the eternal life which God giveth unto all the obedient.' (Moses 5:11) If it hadn't been for Eve, none of us would be here." *(James E. Faust, "What it Means to Be a Daughter of God" Oct 1999 General Relief Society Meeting)*

Eve and Esther are incredible examples of living life to the fullest. Our mortal experience will be what we decide it will be. We have agency – something we fought for in the pre-Earth life. This means whether we squander our mortality or soak up every moment of it, good, hard, happy, sad – it is our choice.

These chapters have covered a whole array of implementing the motto YOLO in our lives. My daughter's personal letter to her baby boy is a good reminder for all of us:

> *When confronted with that daunting question, "What are you going to name your baby?" Steven and I thought it more polite to say, "We haven't decided yet," rather than, "It's a secret which will not be revealed until the birth of our child." Not that we were trying to drum up anticipation or anything like that. We just felt that both names we had picked out (we let the gender be a surprise this time around) had so much personal meaning that we wanted to keep them close.*

> *When I found out that I was pregnant last May, I was elated. But in just a few short weeks, everything became all fuzzy and weird. The thing is, we hadn't been planning on getting pregnant. I can't tell you how excited I was that our third child would come without lots and lots of waiting, trying, hoping, praying, and all of the other rocky torrents that seem to accompany me and pregnancy. I felt like I was walking on a cloud and then when the ultrasound offered little hope that the baby would live, I felt like an idiot. Of course I was going to miscarry. Why wouldn't I? Why had I ever convinced myself that I could just be "normal" and have a surprise pregnancy?*

And so on and so on.

It was June at this point and summers in upstate New York are beautiful and green. There are ripe berries to be picked, blue skies and sandy beaches less than an hour away from wherever you are. But I didn't really exist that summer. I was not only on bedrest, hoping to give the baby a fighting chance, but I was also having a major IC flair-up that took the fight out of me. When I think about last summer, I see myself watching my kids play in the backyard with my mom and sister (who saved us) from my bedroom window.

It was hard. It was stressful. Every doctor's appointment was like a slap in the face and I could barely stand the constant, aching worry inside of me. I knew that I had reached my own rock-bottom when the only thing I could muster enough will to do was to lie on my couch after the kids had gone to bed and listen to "High and Dry" by Radiohead on repeat. Low point.

In September I was listening to a talk by Jeffrey R. Holland (Place No More for the Enemy of my Soul, April 2010 General Conference) and with just five words, I was thrown out of my pit of self-pity and fear.

"Let will be your reason."

The realization crashed over me that over the past months: my own will hadn't governed anything. I'd allowed myself to be forced into a place where fear and pain dictated my every thought and action.

Was my own will enough, though? Just because I willed it, could I be happy? Even with the burdens that were so very heavy to me?

A resounding yes echoed through my being and just like that, the cold winter of my soul melted into the sweet sunset-orange of fall, and life was good again.

Will, you were given your name so that you would always remember to let will be your reason. Your own will is stronger than any feeling, habit, passion, pressure, physical ailment - the list goes on and on - your will is stronger than all of it.

Always choose what you do, what you think, how you react, who you are. Act, never be acted upon.

Choose your life, Will.

"In the depth of winter, I finally learned that there was in me an invincible summer." (Albert Camus)

My will to choose hope instead of despair reminded me of my own invincible summer. When you are in a place where hope seems far away and unreachable, choose to fight for it until it fills you up.

The thought of you - bundled in warm blankets, sleeping on my chest in the early hours of the morning, curled little fists in your lap - thoughts that I accepted might never materialize but were nevertheless beautiful and real to me - saved me. You were my reason.

May we all remember that *You Only Live Once* in mortality, and we each choose to make what we will of our moments. YOLO.

Many thanks to Jennilyn Call Eckersley for her
meticulous editing and creative advice!

DenaleeChapman.com